Terrorism and Justice

Moral Argument in
a Threatened World

EDITED BY

C. A. J. (Tony) Coady and
Michael P. O'Keefe

MELBOURNE UNIVERSITY PRESS

MELBOURNE UNIVERSITY PRESS
an imprint of Melbourne University Publishing (MUP Ltd)
PO Box 1167, Carlton, Victoria 3053, Australia
mup-info@unimelb.edu.au
www.mup.com.au

First published 2002
Reprinted 2003

Typeset in Malaysia by Syarikat Seng Teik Sdn. Bhd.
Printed in Australia by Openbook Print

National Library of Australia Cataloguing-in-Publication entry

Terrorism and justice: moral argument in a threatened world.

  Bibliography.
  Includes index.
  ISBN 0 522 85049 9.

  1. Terrorism. I. Coady, C. A. J. (Tony). II. O'Keefe,
  Michael P.
303.625

Publication of this work was assisted by a publication
grant from the University of Melbourne.

Terrorism and
Justice

Ethics in Public Life

This series aims to provide intellectually challenging treatments of the ethical dimensions of issues of public importance. The perspective is broadly philosophical, in that issues are examined with a view to their basic presuppositions and underlying fundamental values. The series is edited by Professor C. A. J. (Tony) Coady, Head of the University of Melbourne division of the Australian Research Council Special Research Centre for Applied Philosophy and Public Ethics.

Other titles in the series are:

Codes of Ethics and the Professions, edited by Margaret Coady and Sidney Bloch, 1996.

All Connected: Universal Service in Telecommunications, edited by Bruce Langtry, 1998.

Violence and Police Culture, edited by C. A. J. (Tony) Coady, Steve James, Seumas Miller and Michael P. O'Keefe, 2000.

Contents

Contributors

Professor C. A. J. (Tony) Coady is an Australian Research Council Senior Research Fellow in Philosophy at the University of Melbourne. He is Head of the University of Melbourne division of the Australian Research Council Special Research Centre for Applied Philosophy and Public Ethics. He has published extensively in both academic and more general venues, and is a frequent commentator on public issues in the media. His book, *Testimony: A Philosophical Inquiry* (1992), was widely and enthusiastically reviewed in Europe and America as well as in Australia. He recently co-edited *Violence and Police Culture* (MUP, 2000).

Raimond Gaita is Professor of Philosophy at the Australian Catholic University, Melbourne, and Professor of Moral Philosophy at the University of London, King's College. He is widely published in academic and more general publications, and has contributed extensively to discussion of matters of public concern. His books include *Good and Evil: An Absolute Conception* (1991), *Romulus, My Father* (1998), *A Common Humanity: Thinking About Love & Truth & Justice* (1999), and *The Philosopher's Dog* (2002).

Seumas Miller is Director of the ARC Centre for Applied Philosophy and Public Ethics, and is Head of the Philosophy Program at Charles Sturt University, Canberra. Professor Miller's recent publications include *Police Ethics* (1997) with Andrew Alexandra and John Blackler; *Violence and Police Culture* (MUP, 2000), co-edited with Tony Coady, Steve James and Michael O'Keefe; and *Social Action: A Teleological Account* (2001).

Michael P. O'Keefe is a Research Fellow in the ARC Centre for Applied Philosophy and Public Ethics, University of Melbourne. His research interests include the ethics of humanitarian intervention, military and police ethics and Australia's defence and security policies. He also teaches in politics and defence studies at La Trobe University and Deakin University. He co-edited *Violence and Police Culture* (MUP, 2000).

Aleksandar Pavković is Associate Professor in Politics at Macquarie University, Sydney, and an Honorary Senior Research Fellow at the ARC Centre for Applied Philosophy and Public Ethics, University of Melbourne. In his *The Fragmentation of Yugoslavia: Nationalism and War in the Balkans* (2000), and a series of essays on the Serb and on the pan-Yugoslav national ideas, he examined the role of national liberation ideologies in the recent conflict in this region. He has also written on Thomas More's utopian vision and on the idea of supranational European identity. His current research is concerned with contemporary theories of national self-determination and of secession.

Igor Primoratz is Associate Professor of Philosophy at the Hebrew University, Jerusalem, and Principal Research Fellow at the ARC Centre for Applied Philosophy and Public Ethics, University of Melbourne. He is the author of *Justifying Legal Punishment* (1989, 1997) and *Ethics and Sex* (1999), and of numerous papers in moral, political, and legal philosophy. Publications on terrorism and related topics include 'What Is Terrorism?' (*Journal of Applied Philosophy*, 1990), 'The Morality of Terrorism' (ibid., 1997), and 'Michael Walzer's Just War Theory: Some Issues of Responsibility' (*Ethical Theory and Moral Practice*, 2002).

Abdullah Saeed is Associate Professor and Head of Arabic and Islamic Studies Program at the University of Melbourne. He holds a BA in Arabic and Islamic Studies from Saudi Arabia, a PhD in Islamic Studies and a Masters degree in Applied Linguistics, both from the University of Melbourne. His research interests include modern Islamic thought, Islamic hermeneutics and Islam in Australia. Among his recent publications are *Islamic Banking and Interest* (1999), *Muslim Communities in Australia* (co-edited, 2001) and *Freedom of Religion, Apostasy and Islam* (in press).

Sir Ninian Stephen is a former High Court judge and Governor-General of Australia. He was appointed in 1992 by the United

Kingdom and Republic of Ireland governments as chairman of Strand Two of the Talks on Northern Ireland. He was also a judge on the United Nations International Criminal Tribunal for the former Yugoslavia from 1993 to 1997.

Janna Thompson is an Associate Professor in Philosophy at La Trobe University, Melbourne, and a Principal Research Fellow in the ARC Centre for Applied Philosophy and Public Ethics, University of Melbourne. She is the author of *Justice and World Order* (1992), *Discourse and Knowledge* (1997), and *Taking Responsibility for the Past* (2002).

Robert Young teaches Philosophy at La Trobe University, Melbourne. He is the author of *Freedom, Responsibility and God* (1975), and *Personal Autonomy: Beyond Negative and Positive Liberty* (1986), and papers on ethics, politics and religious belief. He is also completing a book on decision making in relation to death and dying. He is a Fellow of the Academy of Humanities of Australia.

Acknowledgements

The editors would like to acknowledge the support of the Australian Research Council Special Research Centre for Applied Philosophy and Public Ethics. The Centre sponsored the workshop from which the work grew, and supported much of the research that went into the final form of the book. Our thanks also to Irena Blonder and Lisa Ball for their help with the organisation of the workshop. Thanks are also due to Toni Morton, Research Assistant at CAPPE, who provided invaluable editorial assistance during the preparation of the manuscript for publication; and to Will Barrett for help with the index.

Earlier versions of Raimond Gaita's chapter appeared in the *Age*, 20 October 2001, and in Peter Craven (ed.), *The Best Australian Essays 2001* (Black Inc, Melbourne, 2001). Our thanks to them for permission to re-use material from those publications.

Preface

TERRORISM IS BOTH palpable and elusive. We are confronted by it, haunted by it, and confused about it. In some form or another it is as old as the sense of civilisation that it threatens, but its manifestations can be as novel as the latest fashion in weaponry. In the wake of 11 September 2001 and the October 12 Bali bombing the technologically advanced Western states are sensitive to it as never before, but other parts of the world are wearily familiar with its ravages. Sri Lankans, Irish, English, South Africans, Palestinians, Israelis, Indonesians, have all lived with its constant strain. From this perspective, the idea that the outrages of September 11 were somehow unique or changed the world forever can be seen as understandable exaggeration. They certainly wrought an enormous change in the consciousness of Americans and, to some extent, of the inhabitants of other affluent countries such as Australia. Americans, in particular, have lost a sense of invulnerability that had been growing since the end of the Cold War, and this has naturally created the temptation to panic. In the world's sole superpower, possessed of astonishing military and economic capacities, any degree of panic is cause for concern. Washington's prescription of open-ended 'war on terror' can only heighten this concern. This concern is increased by the ways in which the events of September 11 have already influenced political crises around the world. The most notable were the severe Israeli responses to Palestinian terrorism in April 2002, responses that were themselves subject to the allegation of terrorism. Notable also is the disturbing tendency in some quarters to view the threat of terrorism as coming from the whole Moslem world. All of which makes it important to take a hard look at the moral and conceptual issues surrounding terrorism.

This book represents a contribution to that task of scrutiny and evaluation. It is written predominantly by philosophers, though it includes chapters by an eminent jurist, a political scientist, and an Islamic scholar. Several of the contributors were participants in a workshop run by the Melbourne division of the Australian Research Council Special Research Centre for Applied Philosophy and Public Ethics at the University of Melbourne in November 2000. The contributors have tried to examine the vexed matters of defining terrorism, assessing the moral status of resort to terrorism, the international legal regime most suited to dealing with it, the role of state terrorism, the role of an ideology of liberation in defending terrorism, the idea of collective responsibility and its function in licensing violent attacks, the issue of whether terrorism is more like war than like crime, and the specifics of the attitudes underlying the contemporary responses to terrorism.

The chapters by Coady, Primoratz, Young and Stephen devote most attention to answering the question: What is terrorism? Any definitional answer inevitably involves a degree of stipulation since the term 'terrorism' figures in so much polemics and propaganda. Partly for this reason, Young prefers to leave it undefined, though he lists several marks that he takes to be characteristic. Coady, Primoratz and Stephen, on the other hand, reach a degree of non-collusive unanimity in defining terrorism as a certain sort of tactic in the use of political violence; namely, the directing of such violence at innocent people. Of course, the word 'innocent' needs a lot more attention and gets a good deal of it in some of the chapters. Coady prefers 'non-combatant', Stephen speaks of the 'defenceless' and Primoratz of 'the innocent'. On the moral assessment issue, Young is worried that definitions of this kind stack the decks against any possible moral justification of terrorism. Thompson seems to share this worry. But Primoratz thinks that, so defined, terrorism may nonetheless be justified *in extremis*, and Coady thinks the definition leaves room for a case to be made for terrorism but that the case is unpersuasive, even in 'supreme emergency'. In any event, on the face of it, if terrorism is impermissible it must be impermissible for states as well as sub-state groups; conversely, if it permissible for sub-state groups it must also be allowed for states on the same or similar terms.

The issue of moral assessment raises the question of a framework for assessment. Most of the contributors who confront this question have recourse, to greater or less extent, to the tradition of 'just war' thinking. Thompson argues the need for modifications to the tradition, and it lies in the background to Gaita's argument. Pavkovic, however, describes a tradition he calls liberation humanism, apparently at odds with just war thinking, and contrasts it with what he names universal humanism that plausibly includes just war thinking.

Several of the contributors consider the issue of state terrorism (Primoratz most extensively) and there is generally agreement that states not only can sponsor terrorism by non-state groups but that states can, and do, directly engage in terrorism. Coady instances the terror bombings of World War II, including Hiroshima and Nagasaki, as acts of terrorism, and Primoratz provides a more extensive list. Terrorists of all sorts frequently resort to the idea that the apparent innocents they attack are not really innocent because they are guilty by association. Their membership in certain groups ('oppressors' in Pavkovic's exposition) makes them responsible for the evils that the group leaders or persecuting members perpetrate, and hence liable for retaliatory violence. Pavkovic sees this thesis as a pivotal claim in the liberationist ideology he explores. Miller more generally investigates the idea of collective responsibility, shows the inadequacy of typical terrorist accounts of it, and sets limits to the notion's applicability. These limits apply to both state and non-state terrorist activities.

An urgent question raised by terrorist attacks is that of appropriate response. This has both moral and pragmatic dimensions, and several papers explore these issues. Stephen looks at the legal resources for dealing with terrorism; O'Keefe explores the ways in which international terrorism tempts states to resort to unconstrained counterterrorism, and he offers suggestions about the morally appropriate responses they should make to the threat; Thompson raises questions about the legal treatment of captured terrorists or suspects; and Gaita surveys moral and philosophical dimensions of crucial international events influenced by responses to the September 11 disaster. He offers wide-ranging reflections on the language of anti-terrorist rhetoric, and its connection and disconnection with the deeper reaches of moral understanding.

Several other contributors reject the language in which the response to terrorism is commonly couched. This language has escalated in extravagance and unreality since September 11 and Bali. Phrases that locate evil as wholly other, and good as wholly present in the speakers or their nations, distort perception and make it difficult to comprehend moral and political realities. Where the enemy is portrayed solely in terms of satanic evil and one's own people as the purveyors of 'infinite justice' through military might, the scene is set for the sort of delusional thinking that hinders understanding of the motivations of opponents and vitiates policies for dealing with them. It also distorts false consciousness about one's own record on terrorism. No nation is unblemished by the propensity to terrorism: the United States remains the only state to have used nuclear weapons on civilian populations, and its state agencies have supported the extensive use of terrorism in South America and elsewhere. Blinkered simplification has also been particularly powerful in the understanding of Islamic religious attitudes to violence. As Saeed shows in his sensitive exposition of the intricacies of traditional Islamic theorising about jihad, the simplification has been present in the thinking and rhetoric of both Muslim terrorists and those who aim to hunt them down. Since the religious impulse certainly played a role in the September 11 terrorist attacks on America, the Bali bombings and indeed in some of the fundamentalist rhetoric of the immediate American responses to it ('crusade', 'infinite justice'), there is a pressing need to examine closely the relevant religious traditions. Saeed's chapter is a significant contribution to this examination.

Since the tragic events of 11 September 2001 and 12 October 2002 much remains opaque about the role of terrorism in the future of our violent world. The 'war on terror' continues with no end in sight. The stated aim of the war, the destruction of Al Qaeda, has not been achieved and new threats from terrorist groups are being identified with alarming regularity. Another disturbing development is that war against Iraq is being linked to the 'war on terror'. But there is a widespread conviction that this link is tenuous at best. Moreover, public opinion is deeply divided about the wisdom of intervention in Iraq. There is a real prospect that this divisive atmosphere may undermine the international consensus that is needed to deal justly with the real dangers of international terrorism. It is our hope that the scrutiny of the issues raised and canvassed in this book will stimulate the sort of discussion that is needed to help us all see more clearly the way forward.

March 2003

1

Toward a Definition of Terrorism[1]

Ninian Stephen

Suddenly, on 11 September 2001, the familiar world we had been inhabiting changed in significant ways, changed not only in innumerable ways affecting our daily lives but changed too in how we evaluated our own actions and reactions to world events and the complex reactions of others around us. I suspect that we can never again regard ourselves as relatively immune from the traumas to which many countries have had to become accustomed. Certainly this is the theme of which we hear so much from the United States, which can no longer contemplate as a possible national strategy retirement into safe though solitary isolation.

Central to this extraordinary shift in world events is terrorism, yet a curiosity about terrorism is the absence of agreement as to what is and is not terrorism. This is in itself strange enough. We have known terrorism for centuries and thousands of books and articles in scholarly journals have had aspects of terrorism as their theme; but one thing this great debate on terrorism has not produced is agreement about a definition of terrorism. In the literature there exist innumerable definitions of terrorism, but no general consensus.

As is well known, the nations of the world have over the past almost one hundred and fifty years managed to arrive at some general agreement about some rules of warfare, and how it should be waged, although these rules are fragile things, easily falling apart under the stress of conflict. These rules are expressed in Hague Rules, in Geneva Conventions and in relatively recent United Nations (UN) treaties and conventions, and are replete with definitions, but there remains a problem in the case of terrorism.

It would be worthwhile for the world to devote some time and care to the ascertainment of a generally acceptable definition of terrorism, so that, measured against that definition, it will be possible, as, for instance, with piracy and slave trading, to readily and beyond doubt declare a particular act to be one of terrorism, and accordingly contrary to generally accepted international law. The hoped-for consequence would be that such an act would be treated by all nations as internationally criminal, regardless of their particular view of the government against which the terrorist act was aimed. The price of reaching such a consensus may be the adoption of a quite narrow definition, but that is a price well worth paying. So long as universal agreement is absent, there are likely to remain nation-state havens for terrorists to which they can flee, perhaps taking hostages with them, and from which they can certainly plan future attacks and obtain weapons and all the apparatus of terrorism.

If terrorism of its nature at least includes, although not being confined to, political movements that systematically employ the creation of widespread fear in order to attain their goals, we can identify very early examples. The Jewish zealots of the first and second century who made their last desperate stand against Hadrian's Roman legions at Massada beside the Dead Sea; the Assassins, Islamic radicals of a thousand years later; and then, another eight hundred years on, the most famous of all, at least until recent years—the Russian terrorists of the late eighteenth and nineteenth centuries, were all fanatics and idealists who employed terror as their weapon. By the nineteenth century terrorists had been blessed by the invention of dynamite. The advent of dynamite at one stroke made possible the doctrine of propaganda by deed, the bomb becoming in anarchist eyes the people's friend. It made everyone at last equal in potential for effective violence, which now was no longer the monopoly of the state.

The Russian terrorists of the eighteenth and nineteenth century drew their inspiration from the long literature of tyrannicide, the justifiable killing of a tyrant ruler, a literature that flourished in the city states of ancient Greece. Later Seneca wrote that no victim is more agreeable to god than the blood of a tyrant. However, the problem with tyrannicide and its justification has always been to distinguish between tyrant and lawful ruler; and a problem similar in quality affects any discussion of terrorism: how to distinguish between the criminal terrorist and the violent but heroic freedom fighter.

It is worth noting in passing that, in what seems a very unfair result, it tends to be in open, pluralistic democracies rather than in totalitarian societies that terrorism does best, particularly in terrorism's early manifestations, before the forces of order have developed any long experience in dealing with it. On the other hand, the last hundred years has shown that in totalitarian states of left and right the terrorist has little prospect of successful operation. The police state, where control of populations is pervasive, with movement restricted, identification demanded at every turn, and employment and housing closely monitored, is no place for a terrorist group.

There is, of course, another potent factor favouring an open society as a theatre of operation in the eyes of the terrorist, and that is the existence of its unfettered media. Both high policy of the terrorist group and personal vanity of the individual terrorist will dictate that wide publicity should be given to acts of terrorism—their very purpose is to create fear and confusion and, through it, capitulation to demands, and this makes media coverage an essential. Only in an open society can this be had.

One of the key factors in the failure to date of international accord on action against terrorism has been over-ambitious aims. Closely linked to this has been the injection into the dialogue of ideological elements; one man's, or one government's, freedom fighter being all too often another's terrorist.

The progress to date on attaining anything like general international agreement on the suppression of terrorism has been slight. There have been both bilateral and multilateral efforts to achieve agreement, but full-scale multilateral efforts at suppression of terrorism have been largely unsuccessful. In the case of the hijacking of aircraft, for example, three conventions on civil aviation—in Tokyo in 1963, the Hague in 1970 and Montreal in 1971—sought in vain to impose an effective worldwide regimen, with a universally observed obligation on the country of refuge to extradite or prosecute. The stumbling blocks have included the political offence exception to extradition, the existence of widely different legal systems, the jealous guarding of sovereignty, difficulties of evidence when the crime is international in its elements and the absence of international sanctions against a nation which fails to observe the extradite or prosecute obligation.

Of UN action against terrorism, the words of Walter Laqueur may not be unduly harsh. He saw UN deliberations as 'of no consequence'.[2] As some authors have noted, UN attempts to combat terrorism have had little effect, and UN initiatives seem to be contradictory because of fundamental disagreements among member-states over whether terrorist acts could be justified as acts of national liberation.[3] This is made the more confusing by the absence of agreed definition of these two emotion-charged descriptions.

The members of the European Community (EC), sharing relatively common interests and approaches, have been perhaps the most successful at agreed action on international terrorism. The Council of Europe concluded the European Convention on the Suppression of Terrorism in 1977, its prime purpose being to establish the prosecute or extradite principle for terrorist acts, doing away with the political defence answer to extradition applications. This was then followed up by the European Community's Dublin Agreement of 1979, which seeks to have the 1977 European convention apply without qualification as between EC member-states in extradition proceedings.

International agreement on the suppression of terrorism seems inevitably to run up against either ideological difficulties or conflicts of national strategic or trading interests or both. This is, in a sense, inherent in the nature of terrorism, in the fact that its ultimate target is a particular nation's government, and its aim is the overthrow of that government's authority and legitimacy. Other governments will almost certainly have strong feelings about that challenge, either pro or con, depending on matters of ideology and national interest. Those feelings will then colour the view they take of the means used by any group of activists to challenge the authority of a government, influencing the judgement as to whether the means are terroristic and ought to be branded as internationally criminal or legitimate and internationally acceptable.

Any hope of international consensus on the suppression of terrorism depends first of all upon avoiding the notion of inherently *good* and *bad* governments as providing any yardstick for identifying what is or is not terrorism. What are good and bad governments depends very much on the eye of each beholder nation.

Ruling out then, the *nature* of the regime under attack as any worthwhile criterion of terrorism as an internationally recognised crime, there are other feasible criteria of terrorism that concern themselves in one way or another, not with the regime attacked but rather with aspects of the attack itself. If the attack is examined, three distinct elements emerge: the quality of the particular act of violence, the motive for perpetrating it, and the identity of the victims, that is, the persons or items of property that directly suffer.

The first two of these, the quality of the act and its motive, seem to me to be relatively useless as distinguishing marks of internationally criminal conduct so long as the world community continues to recognise that an attempt to overthrow a particular regime should not of itself be an international crime. Whatever test of criminality is to be applied, it must surely not be one that would stifle all revolutionary movements, seeking merely to perpetuate the existing status quo worldwide. Any proposed rule that tends to set in concrete the global status quo in nation-states would be neither morally nor, I suspect, in the long run politically acceptable. In any acceptable international law, there must surely be room for revolutionaries and separatists, just as there should be no toleration of terrorists.

And the trouble with both the quality of the particular act of violence and the motive for it as tests of what is unacceptable terrorism is that neither is sufficiently discriminating. The patriot rebel, the noble revolutionary, will at times employ the same violent means as those whom we would wish to label as internationally criminal. Examination of motive has never seemed to me to be particularly useful, and of course the suicide bombers and plane hijackers of recent times have made motive a quite inappropriate criterion, unless one were to classify fanaticism in religious belief as in itself involving criminality. Religious fanatics apart, among freedom fighters and terrorists alike there will be many who, according to their own lights, act from the purest of motives. To seek in either the *quality* of the act of violence or the *motive* for it the test of what is at all likely to be universally accepted internationally as criminal terrorism seems to me to be vain. The old stumbling block of one man's freedom fighter, another's terrorist, applies to each of these criteria.

Not so, however, if one adopts what I have described as the third element of an act of violence, namely the identity of the victim. It does afford a criterion that appears to be both viable and likely to appeal to nations worldwide as a valid test of what is internationally unacceptable, and hence properly to be treated as internationally criminal. And, if ever anything can spur the nations of the world into effective action clearly to unite in defining what amounts to terrorism and declaring it a recognised international crime, the events of September 11 surely should.

I suggest that a viable criterion of terrorism, identifying it in terms likely to prove universally acceptable, which is absolutely essential if it is to be of any utility, is the quality of the *victims* of a violent act.

I would propose, as a workable criterion, the defencelessness of the victim. It is a test not without difficulty, the difficulty of deciding who is *defenceless* in that sense; but it does seem to offer prospects of general acceptance. It has appeal on grounds of generally accepted standards of morality worldwide; its simple argument that the defenceless should be protected from extraneous violence should assist in its acceptance. The definition of defenceless victim is, of course, not easy. In this area nothing is easy. The military, and the police, both of them whether in or out of uniform, on or off duty, and, I rather think, also political leaders and high functionaries of state, I would be inclined to exclude from the category of defenceless victims, if only because in seeking global consensus a modest beginning should be made. Ordinary unarmed citizens, on the other hand, even if they be enthusiastic supporters of the government under attack, I would unquestionably include in the category of defenceless. There will, of course, be shadowy areas of doubt and difficult boundary lines to be defined and drawn; but matters of degree always arise in cases of this sort and solutions to them are not beyond the wit of mankind. Attacks upon defenceless victims or those which recklessly involve them, whether by killing or injuring them or taking them hostage or destroying their property, would then become simply criminal as a matter of accepted international law, with all nations being obliged either to try and punish the terrorist responsible if the crime was within their territory or extraditing them to the territory where the crime was committed, for trial there.

The effect of such a rule would be that neither nobility of motive nor justice of the cause would legitimate such violent acts. Like pirates, the perpetrators would be international outlaws, and every civilised state would deny them refuge or aid, and in turn would prevent its citizens from offering them either.

Wholly domestic terrorism could be left to one side; it needs no international action but can be left to local laws to deal with like any other criminal conduct. Also unnecessary to deal with would be cases that really amount to the acts of nation-states, using a group of terrorists as their surrogate. This would be no proper area for international agreement on terrorism but, rather, a case of hostile national conduct under another guise, to be dealt with as nations have always dealt with the hostile acts of other states, by protest, by severance of relations, by show of force, or, in extreme cases, by recourse to war.

The course being taken at present, centred upon Afghanistan and Osama bin Laden, is to describe what is in question as a war against terrorism. The enormity of the attacks on New York and Washington no doubt account for the term war, but to dignify them as acts of war is to give them more than their due. They are simply terrorism, and should be dealt with as international crimes rather than as matters of warfare. An international definition of criminal terrorism that would fix, as its identifying character, upon the violent act against the defenceless victim would clearly apply to the present case, and would be a criterion likely to be acceptable to all the nations of the world. A clear definition seems to me to be an essential first step in the creation of an effective international sanction against terrorism.

This proposed regimen for the suppression of international terrorism has modest aims, hedged about as it is with a restrictive definition and with exclusions, but that is still better than what exists today. Only by such a modest beginning, by aiming at something that all nations will feel able to agree upon as truly inexcusable, and hence properly to be treated universally as internationally criminal, does there seem to be any prospect of creating an internationally recognised offence of terrorism that will have real meaning.

2

Terrorism, Just War and Supreme Emergency

C. A. J. (Tony) Coady

What is terrorism?

Defining terrorism is a hazardous task. It has been estimated that there are well over one hundred different definitions of terrorism in the scholarly literature.[1] This disarray reflects the highly polemical contexts in which the term is used so that the act of defining can become a move in a campaign rather than an aid to thought. Consider some influential definitions picked out by the Terrorism Research Center in the United States.

1   'Terrorism is the use or threatened use of force designed to bring about political change' (Brian Jenkins).
2   'Terrorism constitutes the illegitimate use of force to achieve a political objective when innocent people are targeted' (Walter Laqueur, *The Age of Terrorism*).
3   'Terrorism is the premeditated, deliberate, systematic murder, mayhem, and threatening of the innocent to create fear and intimidation in order to gain a political or tactical advantage, usually to influence an audience' (James M. Poland, *Understanding Terrorism*).
4   'Terrorism is the unlawful use or threat of violence against persons or property to further political or social objectives. It is usually intended to intimidate or coerce a government, individuals or groups, or to modify their behaviour or politics' (Vice-President's Task Force, 1986).
5   'Terrorism is the unlawful use of force or violence against persons or property to intimidate or coerce a government, the civilian population, or any segment thereof, in furtherance of political or social objectives' (FBI Definition).[2]

We might note that Jenkins's definition has the consequence that all forms of war are terrorist. Whatever verdict we give on war, it is surely just confusing to equate all forms of it, including the armed resistance to Hitler, with terrorism. More interestingly, several of the definitions make use of the idea of unlawful or illegitimate violence, but this seems to fudge too many questions about what is wrong with terrorism. The idea of the illegal simply raises the issue of what and whose laws are being broken—armed internal resistance to Hitler by German citizens would arguably have been justified, yet it would certainly have been against German law. And the adjective illegitimate needs unpacking in terms of what makes this or that use of force illegitimate.

Rather than further reviewing the varieties of definition, I propose to concentrate on one key element in common responses to and fears about terrorism, namely the idea that it involves 'innocent' victims. This element features in several of the quoted definitions. It was recently overtly invoked by Yasser Arafat's condemnation of terrorism when he said: 'no degree of oppression and no level of desperation can ever justify the killing of innocent civilians. I condemn terrorism, I condemn the killing of innocent civilians, whether they are Israeli, American or Palestinian'.[3] It also usefully provides a point of connection with the moral apparatus of just war theory, specifically the principle of discrimination and its requirement of non-combatant immunity. Of course, terrorism does not always take place in the context of all-out international war, but it usually has a warlike dimension. I will define it as follows: 'the organised use of violence to target non-combatants ("innocents" in a special sense) for political purposes'.

This definition has several contentious consequences. One is that states can themselves use terrorism, another is that much political violence by non-state agents will not be terrorist. As to the former, there is a tendency, especially among the representatives of states, to restrict the possibility of terrorist acts to non-state agents. But if we think of terrorism, in the light of the definition above, as a tactic rather than an ideology, this tendency should be resisted, since states can and do use the tactic of attacking the innocent. This is why allegations of terrorism against Israeli government forces in parts of Palestine during the anti-terrorist campaign in 2002 made perfect sense, even if the truth of the claims was contentious.

Some theorists who think terrorism cannot be perpetrated by governments are not so much confused as operating with a different definition. They define terrorism, somewhat in the spirit of the FBI definition, as the use of political violence by non-state agents against the state. Some would restrict it to violence against a democratic state. This is the way many political scientists view terrorism. Call this the political definition to contrast with the tactical definition.

A further consequence of the tactical definition is that it implies a degree of purposiveness that terrorism is thought to lack. Some theorists have claimed that terrorism is essentially 'random', others that it is essentially 'expressive'. In both cases, the claim is that a reference to political purposes is inappropriate. In reply, it can be argued that talk of terrorism as random is generated by the genuine perception that it does not restrict its targets to the obvious military ones, but this does not mean that it is wild and purposeless. Indeed, most terrorists think that the best way to get certain political effects is to aim at 'soft' non-combatant targets. Similarly, there can be no doubt that many terrorist attacks are expressive and symbolic, involving the affirmation of the attitude: 'We are still here; take notice of us'. Yet the expressive need not exclude the purposive. So terrorist acts can be, and usually are, both expressive and politically purposive. It is a further question whether these purposes are particularly realistic. The idea that terrorist acts are merely expressive is partly sustained by the belief that when viewed as purposive the acts are basically futile. The futility is often real enough, but purposive acts abound that are in fact futile. Note that I am not *defining* terrorism as immoral: it needs discussion and some background moral theory to show that it is immoral.

The just war tradition

It is time to say a few words about the just war tradition that provides much of that background. Its development has been strongly influenced by Catholic philosophers and theologians in the West, but also by people of quite different commitments, such as Aristotle, Grotius, Locke, and in modern times Michael Walzer, a non-religious Jew. There are also parallel lines of thought in the ancient Chinese philosophical traditions. This is not surprising, because, unless one takes the view that war is entirely beyond moral concern or that it is simply ruled out by morality, then one has to give some account of what can morally justify it. Just war theories constitute a major line of response to this need; another is provided by utilitarian thinking, and another by the so-called realist tradition. In the just war tradition, this account has two key divisions—the *jus ad bellum* and the *jus in bello*. The former tells us the conditions under which it can be right to resort to war, the latter is concerned to guide us in the permissible methods by which we should wage a legitimate war.

Under the *jus ad bellum* it is common to list the following conditions:

1 War must be declared and waged by legitimate authority.
2 There must be a just cause for going to war.
3 War must be a last resort.
4 There must be reasonable prospect of success.
5 The violence used must be proportional to the wrong being resisted.

Under the *jus in bello* there are basically two governing principles:

1 *The Principle of Discrimination*—this limits the kind of kind of violence that can be used, principally by placing restrictions on what count as legitimate targets.
2 *The Principle of Proportionality*—this limits the degree of response by requiring that the violent methods used do not inflict more damage than the original offence could require.

There are clearly many difficulties with these conditions, but equally clearly they make initial intuitive sense. In this brief discussion, I shall concentrate on the Principle of Discrimination since it is the principle most relevant to my approach to terrorism. As Janna Thompson has noted in Chapter 8 in developing Coates's comments on terrorism, the approach embodied in what I have called 'the political definition' could also connect with just war theory through a particular interpretation of the requirement of legitimate authority.

Moral restrictions on how one conducts oneself in war are apt to be met with incredulity. 'You do what needs to be done to win' is a common response. There is a certain appeal in this pragmatic outlook, but it flies in the face not only of just war thinking but of many common human responses to war. The concept of an atrocity, for instance, has a deep place in our thinking. Even that very tough warrior, the US war ace General Chuck Yeager writes in his memoirs that he suffered genuine moral revulsion at orders to commit 'atrocities' that he was given and complied with in World War II. He was especially 'not proud' of his part in the indiscriminate strafing of a 50 square mile area of Germany that included mainly non-combatants.[4]

A major part of the discrimination principle concerns the immunity of non-combatants from direct attack. This is a key point at which utilitarian approaches to the justification of war tend to clash with the classical just war tradition. Either they deny that the principle obtains at all, or, more commonly, they argue that it applies in virtue of its convenience. The former move is associated with the idea that war is such 'hell' and victory so important that everything must be subordinated to that end, but even in utilitarian terms it is unclear that this form of ruthlessness has the best outcomes, especially when it is shared by the opposing sides. Hence, the more common move is to argue that the immunity of non-combatants is a useful rule for restricting the damage wrought by wars. Non-utilitarians (I shall call them 'intrinsicalists' because they believe that there are intrinsic wrongs, other than failing to maximise good outcomes) can agree that there are such extrinsic reasons for the immunity rule, but they will see this fact as a significant additional reason to conform to the principle. Intrinsicalists will argue that the principle's validity springs directly from the reasoning that licenses resort to war in the first place. This resort is allowed by the need to resist perpetrators of aggression (or, on a broader view, to deal with wrongdoers), and hence it licenses violence only against those who are agents of the aggression.

This prohibition on attacking the non-perpetrators (non-combatants or the innocent as they are often called) has been a consistent theme in the just war tradition. So John Locke says in Chapter XV of his *Second Treatise of Civil Government* that a conqueror with a just cause 'gets no power' over those among the enemy populace who are innocent of waging the war. As Locke puts it: 'they ought not to charged as guilty of the violence and injustice that is committed in an unjust war any farther than they actually abet it'.[5]

It is nonetheless understandable that various questions have been raised about the making of the combatant/non-combatant distinction in the context of modern war. The first point of clarification is that when we classify people as non-combatants or innocents we do not mean that they have no evil in their hearts, nor do we mean that combatants are necessarily full of evil thoughts. The classification is concerned with the role the individual plays in the chain of agency directing the aggression or wrongdoing. And it is agency, not mere cause, that is important since the soldier's aged parents may be part of the causal chain that results in his being available to fight without their having any agent responsibility for what the soldier is doing. The combatant may be coerced to fight, but is still prosecuting the war, even if the greater blame lies with those who coerce. On the other hand, young school-children may be enthusiastic about their country's war, but are not prosecuting it. Neither are the farmers whose products feed the troops, for they would feed them (if they'd buy) whatever their role. It should be added that the combatant/non-combatant distinction is not equivalent to the soldier/civilian distinction even though they overlap considerably. Some civilians, such as political leaders and senior public servants, will be legitimate targets if they are actively directing or promoting unjust violence whether or not they wear uniforms or bear arms.

But even when these distinctions are made there seems room not only for doubt about the application of the distinction to various difficult categories of person such as slave labourers coerced to work in munitions factories but also its applicability at all to the highly integrated citizenry of modern states. Some people say that it is surely anachronistic to think of contemporary war as waged between armies; it is really nation against nation, economy against economy, peoples against peoples. But although modern war has many unusual features, its 'total' nature is more an imposed construction than a necessary reflection of changed reality. Even in World War II not every enemy citizen was a combatant. In any war, there remain millions of people who are not plausibly seen as involved in the enemy's lethal chain of agency. There are, for instance, infants, young children, the elderly and infirm, lots of tradespeople and workers, not to mention dissidents and conscientious objectors. This challenge to the distinction requires there to be no serious moral difference between shooting a soldier who is shooting at you and gunning down a defenceless child who is a member of the same nation as the soldier. The conclusion is perhaps sufficiently absurd or obscene to discredit the argument.

In fact, there has been a remarkable change on this issue in the strategic doctrine and military outlook of many major powers since the end of the Cold War. It is now common to pay at least lip service to the principle, as evidenced by certain restraint shown or announced during the Gulf War, and the bombing of Serbia, and by the widespread condemnation of Russian brutality in Chechnya. The rhetoric, at least, of the recent US-led war in Afghanistan is also respectful of the distinction. The real question is not so much whether it is immoral to target non-combatants (it is), but how 'collateral' damage and death to non-combatants can be defended. This was always a problem in just war theory, often solved by resort to some form of the principle of double effect. This allowed for the harming of non-combatants in some circumstances as a foreseen but unintended side-effect of an otherwise legitimate act of war. The 'circumstances' included the proportionality of the side-effect to the intended outcome. Not everyone agrees with the principle (and this is not the place to discuss it in detail), but the conduct of war in contemporary circumstances is morally impossible unless the activities of warriors are allowed to put non-combatants at risk in certain circumstances. Some modification to the immunity principle to allow indirect harming seems to be in line with commonsense morality in other areas of life, and to be necessitated by the circumstances of war. If it is not available, then pacifism, as Holmes has argued, seems the only moral option.[6]

The tactical definition of terrorism faces the problems already discussed concerning the meaning of the term 'non-combatant', but even more acutely. In guerilla war, for instance, insurgents may not be easily identifiable as combatants, and will seek to enlist or involve the villagers and local inhabitants in the campaign, thereby blurring their status as non-combatants. On the other hand, many state officials who are not directly prosecuting the campaign against the insurgents may be plausibly viewed as implicated in the grievances the revolutionaries are seeking to redress. There are certainly problems here, but they do not seem insurmountable. In the heat and confusion of battle, it may be difficult and dangerous to treat even children as non-combatants, especially where children are coerced or seduced into combatant roles (as is common in many contemporary conflicts). Nonetheless, a premeditated campaign of bombing regional hospitals to induce civilian lack of co-operation with rebels is in palpable violation of the *jus in bello*. So are the murder of infants, and the targeting of state officials, such as water authorities or traffic police, whose roles are usually tangentially related to the causes of the conflict. It is true that some ideologies purport to have enemies so comprehensive as to make even small children and helpless adults 'combatants'. Western advocates of strategic bombing of cities in the name of 'total war' share with the Islamic fanatics who incorporate American air travellers and sundry citizens of Manhattan into their holy targets a simplistic and Manichaean vision of the world. This vision is at odds with the just war tradition's attempt to bring some moral sanity to bear upon the use of political violence.

War, terrorism and 'supreme emergency'

Is terrorism wrong? Given just war theory and the tactical definition, the answer is clearly yes. And if one takes the principle of non-combatant immunity to invoke an absolute moral prohibition, as just war thinkers have commonly done, then it is always wrong. Yet many contemporary moral philosophers, sympathetic to just war thinking, are wary of moral absolutes. They would treat the prohibition as expressing a very strong moral presumption against terrorism and the targeting of non-combatants, but allow for exceptions in extreme circumstances. So, Michael Walzer thinks that in conditions of 'supreme emergency' the violation of the normal immunity is permissible in warfare, though only with a heavy burden of remorse. He thinks the Allied terror bombing of German cities in World War II (in the early stages) was legitimated by the enormity of the Nazi threat. John Rawls has recently endorsed this view while condemning the bombings of Hiroshima and Nagasaki.[7] If this concession is allowed to states, it seems mere consistency to allow it to non-state agents on the same terms. The general reluctance to do so suggests that such categories as 'supreme emergency' may mask contestable political judgements.

Let us look more carefully at this. The idea of exemptions from profound moral constraints has taken many different forms in contemporary moral philosophy. Some of these are closely associated with the philosophy of utilitarianism. In its simplest form, act utilitarianism, and certain allied forms of thought, hold that all moral constraints are simply 'rules of thumb' that can and should be overruled if calculations of the overall outcomes of so doing show that it is productive of more general happiness than sorrow. This seems to me a deeply misguided view of ethics, but I cannot offer a full-scale rebuttal here. Its principal defect in connection with terrorism is that, in essence, it doesn't allow that the profound moral constraints against killing the innocent are really profound at all. That is why it calls them 'rules of thumb', along with all sorts of other shorthand adages in the moral life. In connection with terrorism, the more interesting exemption questions arise for those, like Walzer, who *do* think the restriction profound. Such people don't believe that ordinary calculations of utility can possibly override these sorts of constraints. Nonetheless, they think that certain circumstances can allow the regrettable but morally painful choice to violate such deep norms. Those who think this are sometimes operating in the tradition of what has come to be called 'dirty hands'.[8]

The basic idea, we may here take from the tradition, plausibly traceable to Machiavelli, is that certain necessities of life may require the overriding of profound and otherwise 'absolute' moral prohibitions in extreme situations. Walzer's defence of the terror bombing of German cities in World War II in terms of 'supreme emergency' is clearly in the tradition, and provides a useful focus for discussing its relevance to terrorism. Walzer does not defend the bombing unequivocally. He thinks that, though it was morally wrong as a violation of the principle of discrimination, it was justified by the plea of supreme emergency in the early stages of the war. In the later stages, however, it was just plain morally criminal, since an Allied victory could be reasonably foreseen on the basis of morally legitimate targeting and fighting. The bombing of Dresden was therefore an outright atrocity, though the bombing of other German cities up to 1942 was not. He is clear that the bombing in this earlier phase was a violation of the principle of discrimination, and at one point calls it 'terrorism'. It was morally wrong, and implies guilt, but had to be done.[9]

Walzer's use of the category 'supreme emergency' here is based on the idea that the need to defeat Nazi Germany was no ordinary necessity. Hitler's victory would have been a dire blow to civilisation. The enormity of his regime and its practices was such that his extended empire would have been a disaster for most of the people living under its sway. In addition, the threat of Hitler's victory was present and urgent, and the bombing of German cities aimed directly at the civilian populations was the only offensive weapon the British had.

Now, two things are worth noting about this characterisation. The first is that some of the matters that Walzer factors into this dire judgement on Germany's war efforts were not factors that were known to Churchill and his advisers or influenced the decision to use strategic bombing. Hitler was known to be anti-Semitic and to have persecuted Jews and political opponents, but not to have a program of genocide in hand. So part of the legitimation deployed by Walzer is largely *post facto*. Second, Walzer makes the issue of Germany's possible victory a matter of supreme emergency but not that of Japan. Japan's war, he claims, was 'a more ordinary sort of military expansion, and all that was morally required was that they be defeated, not that they be conquered and totally overthrown'.[10] This is part of his argument against the atomic bombing of Hiroshima and Nagasaki. He denies that this was required by 'supreme emergency', partly because Japan was no longer in a position to win the war so the threat was no longer imminent, and partly because the Japanese did not represent the same danger to civilisation as their Nazi allies. He thinks it mere utilitarianism that the atomic bombs were (allegedly) needed to end the war more quickly with less loss of life, and argues that an ordinary (rather than an unconditional) surrender would have been the morally licit path to ending the war.

A critique of the supreme emergency defence

I hold no brief for the doctrine of unconditional surrender, but Walzer's relatively benign view of Japanese aggression is hard to take seriously. I feel inclined to say: 'Tell that to the Chinese'. In the Japanese invasion of China in the 1930s it is soberly estimated that more than 300 000 Chinese civilians were massacred in Nanking alone in a racist rampage of raping, beheading and bayoneting that lasted six weeks.[11] Nor was the racist and anti-civilisational behaviour of the Japanese warriors much better in the rest of South-East Asia during the war. Those directly threatened with a Japanese victory in Asia and the Pacific would clearly have had a much sounder case for talking of 'supreme emergency' than Walzer allows. Had they had the capacity to terrorise Japanese cities (as the Americans later did), then it would seem that supreme emergency would have licensed their attacking the innocent. But if this is so, then it is hard to resist the suspicion that 'supreme emergency' is too elastic to do the job required. So elastic, indeed, that whenever you are engaged in legitimate self-defence and look like losing you will be able to produce plausible reasons of 'supreme emergency' for attacking the innocent.

A further curiosity of Walzer's argument is that it is presented primarily as an argument available to states and their representatives. This is not exclusively true of the tradition of the 'dirty hands' debate (it is less true of Weber, for instance) but it is a pronounced emphasis of Walzer's treatment. This is particularly surprising, given that Walzer derives the term 'dirty hands' from Sartre's play of the same name, which is concerned with the supposed necessity for revolutionaries to violate morality in pursuit of their cause.[12] But, if we think only of the connotations of 'supreme emergency', it is not at all obvious that the issue can be so restricted. Palestinian resistance groups, for example, can mount a powerful case that they face a hostile power bent upon subordination and dispossession to a degree that threatens not only their lives but their way of life. Even the various groups around Osama bin Laden may well see themselves as qualifying for this exemption. No doubt it can be argued that there are various delusions and mistakes in their outlooks, but the history of warfare is replete with similar delusions and mistakes.

In his discussion of 'supreme emergency' Walzer makes explicit his pro-state bias: 'Can soldiers and statesmen override the rights of innocent people for the sake of their own political communities? I am inclined to answer the question affirmatively, though not without hesitation and worry'.[13] And he goes on to speak of nations in a way that identifies political communities and nations. Of course, even Walzer's language here leaves logical space for the idea that nations or political communities can be driven by necessity, even where they do not possess a state or have been deprived of one. Yet it is clear that recourse by such people or their real or imagined leaders to 'supreme emergency' is far from his mind.

My own view is that the supreme emergency story suffers from grave defects whether it is offered as an exemption on behalf of a state, or some less established political community, or a group claiming to represent either. The first problem is that it undervalues the depth and centrality of the prohibition on killing the innocent. In spite of Walzer's agonising about the need to acknowledge that we have violated an important moral restraint by our bombing or other terror tactic, he locates the prohibition on attacking non-combatants within what he calls 'the war convention'. Although, there is some unclarity about what he means by this, the terminology suggests that the prohibition is itself somehow merely conventional. On the contrary, it is, as I have argued, basic to what makes it legitimate to wage a just war at all. More generally, the prohibition on intentionally killing innocent people functions in our moral thinking as a sort of touchstone of moral and intellectual health. To suspend this, because of necessity or supreme emergency, is to bring about an upheaval in the moral perspective. The situation is, I think, rather like that supposed by the philosopher W. V. O. Quine to operate with empirical and scientific knowledge. Quine thinks that no propositions, even those of logic, are beyond revision or abandonment, but some are more deeply entrenched in our way of thinking and responding to the world than others, and so less revisable. Some indeed may be so deeply entrenched that we cannot imagine what it would be like to have to give them up. Ludwig Wittgenstein makes some similar suggestions in his book *On Certainty*, but explicitly includes many ordinary empirical propositions in the central core.[14] My suggestion is that some of our moral beliefs have an analogous position in the framework of our moral thinking. Rejection of them leads to an unbalance and incoherence in moral thought and practice parallel (though different in kind) to the rejection of entrenched propositions in empirical and theoretical thinking.

My second point is that the primacy of the political community that lies behind much of the dirty hands debate is highly suspect. Walzer admits of individuals that they can never attack innocent people to aid their self-defence.[15] He then adds: 'But communities, in emergencies, seem to have different and larger prerogatives. I am not sure that I can account for the difference, without ascribing to communal life a kind of transcendence that I don't believe it to have'. Walzer goes on to try to locate the 'difference' in the supposed fact that 'the survival and freedom of political communities . . . are the highest values of international society'.[16] Maybe they are the highest values of international society, but this is hardly surprising if one construes international society as a society of political communities, namely recognised states. What is needed, at the very least, is an argument that locates the survival and freedom of political communities as the highest *human* value, and one that is capable of justifying the overriding that 'supreme emergency' requires. I doubt that any such argument exists. Certainly, it is not enough to point to the undoubted value of political life for there are many other values that are equally, if not more, significant.

A third consideration against the dirty hands story in its 'supreme emergency' form is that admission of this exemption is likely to generate widespread misuse of it. On Walzer's own account the 'legitimate' resort to terror in the early stages of World War II led rapidly to its illegitimate use thereafter. It is surely plain enough that the widespread resort to state terror in various contexts has been justified in ways that parallel Walzer's apologetic, and non-state agents are not slow to follow suit. We surely do better to condemn the resort to terrorism outright with no leeway for exemptions, be they for states, revolutionaries or religious zealots.

Moral response

Finally what sorts of violent responses to terrorism can be morally legitimate? The first thing to say of this is that the use of terrorism to combat terrorism should be ruled out. Attacking the innocent is illicit when used by non-state groups and it is wrong when used by states in response. Two wrongs do not make a right. Second, the use of violence to capture or even kill terrorists is legitimate if it accords with the conditions of the *jus ad bellum* that govern the morality of resort to war. One of the crucial conditions most relevant here, and especially relevant to the present 'war against terrorism', is whether the exercise is likely to achieve success. Here it is difficult to know what success amounts to. Venting of rage or grief is hardly sufficient. Bringing the agents of terrorist attack to justice or destroying them would seem a legitimate aim, as would diminishing the future prospect of terrorist attacks. At the time of writing, it is unclear whether the war in Afghanistan has fulfilled these aims. A further campaign of violence against the nations classified by President Bush as forming an 'axis of evil' looks even more problematic from this point of view. It is also doubtful whether it would satisfy the conditions of last resort and proportionality. Finally, and more generally, massive aerial bombardments to aid the military overthrow of ugly regimes is likely to be politically and morally inadequate as a response to terrorism. The paradigm of state-against-state warfare is ill adapted to the threat of terrorists like al-Qaeda since such terrorists are not state-based, are relatively independent of the host nations they infest, and breed on the oppression and injustice in the international order that remain unaddressed by campaigns of violence. Bombing campaigns like that in Afghanistan inevitably produce alarmingly high numbers of non-combatant casualties and damage to civilian infrastructure. Even where these are not directly intended, their scale can betray an immoral indifference to innocent life.

3

Political Terrorism as a Weapon of the Politically Powerless

Robert Young

Because there is so much disagreement about how (political) terrorism should be characterised, it behoves me to begin by setting out how I characterise it. In the process of outlining my characterisation, I will register some disagreement with the positions of some of the other contributors in this volume. Given that the notion is so contested, I will not offer a definition or attempt to provide a set of necessary and sufficient conditions for the correct use of the term since I don't wish to make definitional issues the focus, let alone attempt to rely on a definitional fiat or give the impression that my account is not contested. Instead, I will list the features that, I think, best capture what terrorism involves.

I will focus on terrorism as it is practised by individuals, or groups other than states. It is not my intention to rule out the idea of state terrorism (which will be the subject of a separate chapter).[1] On the contrary, I consider state terrorism to be widely practised. This is a point of importance because state terrorism is not a weapon of the politically powerless (the concern of this chapter), but of the politically powerful.

I will briefly consider the claim that the most promising way, morally, to defend political terrorism other than that carried out by states is to see it as a weapon that those who lack conventional political power can use to fight for just causes they are otherwise prevented from promoting.

Features of terrorism

Terrorist actions (whether in the form of one-off attacks or as part of an ongoing campaign) are political actions that involve either the use, or the threat of the use, of violence. The violence may be directed towards persons or property.[2] That property can be an object of terrorist attack is sometimes denied and often ignored, but examples abound: witness, for example, various of the terrorist attacks on items of infrastructure by the African National Congress in South Africa or the destruction by the Tamil 'Tigers' of much of the fleet of Sri Lankan Airways in 2001. Generally, the violence will take a physical form, but it may also be psychological.

1   The use, or the threat of the use, of violence is intended to generate anxiety, fear, or terror, or to cause a breakdown in normal levels of trust in society, among some target group (even if it is not the persons or property of members of that group that are the direct objects of attack).

2   Those who thus resort to violence may act as individuals, but, more commonly, will be acting as members of an organised group. Individuals or groups other than the state act as insurgents when they resort to terrorism, whereas a state that employs terrorism will do so with a view to upholding its laws or maintaining the political status quo.

3   The purposes for which terrorism is carried out can range from intimidation or coercion of the target group so as to get it to accede to the political demands of the perpetrators, through to obtaining publicity for a cause, the building of morale among members of the attacking group, or even the enforcement of obedience within that group, to attempting to render a territory ungovernable or to provoke a repressive response by the state.[3]

4   Though many claim that terrorism always involves the indiscriminate or random use of violence (and some go so far as to say that it does so necessarily) this need not be the case.[4] Not only can terrorism be directed at property, as was mentioned above, but, as well, it is worth reminding ourselves that warnings of impending terrorist actions are often given so as to preclude needless maiming of individuals who are not targets but happen to be in the vicinity where the action will occur. Moreover, terrorism, at least on some occasions, is directed at specific targets in order to achieve the particular purpose the terrorist intends. It is a general truth that the more indiscriminate a terrorist action the harder it will be to give a moral defence of it (for reasons that will be elaborated later). At least two of the contributors to this book have made

relevantly different claims about these matters in their previous writings on terrorism. C. A. J. Coady, for example, has defined terrorism as 'a political act, ordinarily committed by an organised group, which involves the intentional killing or other severe harming of non-combatants or the threat of the same or intentional severe damage to the property of non-combatants or the threat of the same'.[5] This has the merit that it acknowledges that terrorism may extend to damage to property; however, it begs the question of the moral justifiability of political terrorism. Igor Primoratz takes an even tougher line in that he considers that terrorism necessarily involves the use, or the threat of the use, of violence against 'innocent people'.[6] Surprisingly, he thinks that he has not thereby made moral condemnation of terrorism analytically true[7] but since, like Coady, what he says implies that terrorism is seriously morally wrong, he, too, begs the question.

5   Notwithstanding what I have just said, many believe that terrorism necessarily involves threatening to harm, or harming, non-combatants (which is code for 'innocents'), and so fails to preserve vital distinctions that have been developed through reflection on the morality of violence in war, such as that between combatants and non-combatants. I reject this sort of moralised definition. Not only does a definition of this form beg the question of the moral justifiability of terrorism, it is also unwarrantedly prescriptive about which acts of political violence may be considered acts of terrorism. To take the former first: the definition implies, for instance, that where a terrorist group refrains from giving a warning to enable people to evacuate a building before it is bombed, and casualties are suffered, that an act of terrorism takes place, whereas if warnings are given and no casualties occur there is no act of terrorism but, instead, as some of those who offer such a definition would have it, merely an act of *sabotage*. As regards the latter: consider, for instance, the truck bomb attack in 1983 on the US marine barracks in Lebanon that killed more than 200 soldiers. Lomasky takes the heroic line that the incident was only 'tangentially' a terrorist act. Other cases that have involved the killing, or attempted killing, of individuals whom it is difficult to think of as 'innocent civilians'—like the abduction and killing in 1978 by the Red Brigade of the former Italian Prime Minister, Aldo Moro, or the attempt in

1984 by the Irish Republican Army to kill the then British Prime Minister, Margaret Thatcher, and members of her Cabinet, in their Brighton hotel—have been claimed to constitute *assassinations* or attempted assassinations rather than acts of terrorism. These reclassifications may save the moralised definition but are unhelpful to the careful analysis of the phenomenon of terrorism.

Let us suppose (even if, for some readers, it is only for the sake of argument) that the preceding list of features provides a tolerably clear, non question-begging characterisation of terrorism. That still leaves open to debate whether any particular act of terrorism can be morally justified. So I turn now to a consideration of whether individuals or groups may justifiably resort to terrorism. It is, nonetheless, worth saying in advance that, even on the characterisation I have offered, it will be difficult to provide a convincing moral justification for such violent political action whenever it involves injuring or killing the innocent.

Can terrorism be morally justified?

Such defences of terrorism as there are[8] often begin from the contention that, in at least some circumstances where it is not possible for those with a serious grievance to get the political powers-that-be to give them even a hearing, terrorism may be the only remaining resort. Certain critics, like Michael Walzer,[9] dismiss the contention out of hand by suggesting that it is virtually impossible to reach a final resort because there is always something else that can be tried, even by the most seriously oppressed. (In fairness, Walzer thinks that the same holds for states who, he believes, are altogether too ready to go to war on the pretence of it being their last resort.) Walzer's is a facile response because it amounts to no more than an insistence that however unrealistic, or unlikely to succeed, the remaining options may be, they must continue to be tried. Tell that, for example, to a person from a subjugated minority group suffering serious, systematic violence at the hands of the majority (in recent times, say, those from Kosovo or Aceh), or to the citizens of a country under military occupation by another more powerful nation (say, Cyprus in the 1950s when it was occupied by British forces). Despite the commonly held view of him as exclusively a practitioner of non-violence, and certainly without wanting to suggest that he would have supported terrorism, it is worthy of note that even Gandhi contended that it was 'better to resist oppression by violent means than to submit' in the event that a non-violent response was precluded.[10]

A more promising riposte may be to suggest that the claim, made by those who assert that they must needs resort to terrorism, that they do so because they are politically powerless, relies on a conflation of two very different ideas. On the one hand, there is the claim on the part of a (terrorist) group that the group lacks power as compared with the state they oppose, and, on the other, there is the claim that they lack the ability as a group to obtain and mobilise widespread support for their cause (whether in the form of non-violent resistance, guerrilla warfare or the like).[11] Walzer contends that it is the second claim that we should focus on, whereas I shall suggest that it is the first. He goes on to add that, in a truly despotic and repressive situation, state terrorism will be immune anyway to challenge from revolutionary terrorism or an attempt via terrorism to bring about significant societal reform, whereas, in a democratic setting, other strategies than terrorism will be available; in short, he thinks that, if the cause is just, just means will be available in a democratic context.

Let us consider these claims in reverse order. Even in places where there are some of the trappings of democracy (periodic elections and the like) it may still be very difficult for some groups to get a fair hearing for their grievances. In one of the few places where terrorism could be said to have been a factor in bringing about political change, Northern Ireland,[12] the state was established with a demographic basis that made it likely that the minority section of the population who wished for a unified Ireland would be regularly outvoted by the numerically larger section who wished to remain part of the United Kingdom and, in consequence of being outvoted, be denied access to serious political power and opportunities. (I have chosen to speak of 'the minority section' and the 'numerically larger section' because the use of terms like 'Catholics' and 'Protestants' inaccurately suggests that what is a political struggle is a religious one.) There is, of course, a difference between terrorism proving effective and it being morally justified, but, even with that acknowledged, it may still be that limited forms of terrorism can be justified, even where some of the features of a democracy are present, if getting a fair hearing for serious grievances would otherwise be impossible. Thus, supposing that non-violent options have proved to be to no avail, if the targets are carefully chosen and are confined to property, or to those who cannot reasonably be regarded as innocent, even in a setting with democratic features terrorism may be morally justifiable.[13]

I turn, second, to Walzer's claim that, outside of democratic settings, terrorist tactics are very likely to fail because the state will hold so much political power as to be impregnable from attack. This I simply do not accept. The Irgun Zvi Leumi (the National Military Organization in Palestine) and the Stern Gang used terror tactics against the British rulers of Palestine to achieve a much different political arrangement for the birth of the state of Israel than would otherwise have been the case. The tactic could thus be said to have met with some success.[14] Similarly, terrorist acts carried out by members of the African National Congress (the ANC) were surely among the factors that led to the overthrow of apartheid and the introduction of the more democratic society that is present-day South Africa. In South Africa it was certainly not lack of popular support that rendered black activists politically powerless; it was, manifestly, a lack of power in relation to that of an oppressive state and its institutional apparatus. Not only did the members of the ANC who carried out terrorist acts lack political power, they also claimed to be acting on behalf of the large but politically powerless majority of the population. It is true that, on its own, terrorism would not have brought down the regime, but it played a part in that downfall. Now it is important, as I have said before, to separate the effectiveness of an act of terrorism from its moral justifiability. But, given the horrendous suffering occasioned by the way the system of apartheid operated, some of the ANC's carefully targeted terrorist actions in South Africa seem to be numbered among the morally justified uses of political violence. However, to make that assessment credible, I need to say how it might be supported (at least to the extent that the space available permits).

Does a lack of political power justify resort to terrorism, no matter what?

No, of course, it doesn't. No more, in fact, than does fighting for a just cause by way of war justify whatever is done in the furtherance of that cause. Recourse to war may be just, and so satisfy the *jus ad bellum* (justice of war) standard, without the conduct of the war satisfying the *jus in bello* (justice in war) standard. Many who reject the moral justifiability of terrorism do so because they do not believe that terrorism can measure up to the stringent requirements of the second of these standards. It may be conceded that, like some wars, some acts and even some campaigns of terrorism may be undertaken as a last resort, out of necessity, and have some hope of success. But those staunchly opposed to the moral justifiability of terrorism claim that terrorism cannot satisfy the further and central requirement of the *jus in bello* that any response be proportional. The reason they give is that it is not possible for a response to be proportional if it fails to respect the immunity of non-combatants. Precisely who is entitled to non-combatant status is a subject of dispute within just war theory[15] but there is no need for us to enter that dispute because, as we have already seen, terrorism does not have to involve the targeting of non-combatants. It is also said by some that since terrorism is indiscriminate as to who may be targeted it must fail the further requirement of the *jus in bello* that any violence satisfy the test of discrimination. Again, we have seen that terrorism need not be random and so need not fail this test.

The just war tradition appeals to what philosophers term non-consequentialist considerations. According to non-consequentialists, the rightness or wrongness of what we do is not solely determined by how good or bad the consequences of what we do will be. There are various possible ways of understanding what goodness and badness consist in, but, for present purposes, I will take them to be about how well off or badly off a certain action leaves those whom it affects.[16] Non-consequentialists typically hold that moral judgements must take into account *prerogatives* not to maximise the good (e.g. in the pursuit of our own projects) and *constraints* on producing the best consequences overall (as when doing so would clash with the obligation not to harm others intentionally). Consequentialists, by contrast, hold that the rightness or wrongness of what we do is solely determined by whether what we do maximises good consequences (or, for some recent writers, satisfices, that is, achieves satisfactory, even if less than maximal, good consequences, because to seek to maximise them would require difficult or costly calculations). Clearly, some terrorist actions might be said by consequentialists to be justified because they achieve more good consequences than bad.[17] This is not the occasion to argue a case for either a consequentialist or a non-consequentialist approach to ethics, let alone to consider whether, in particular circumstances, optimally more good than bad might be shown to have come from a terrorist action or campaign. Instead, I will merely state that I am a non-consequentialist who believes, *inter alia*, that the constraints against killing and injuring those not engaged in violent attacks against us may only be set aside when failure to do so would lead to harmful consequences of far greater significance.

For my part, the moral justification for any particular instance of terrorism, or of any political response that includes a campaign of terrorism, will turn on whether justice can be achieved with fewer, and better targeted, killings, injuries and destruction of property, than by any of the other available alternatives (supposing always that all non-violent strategies have been exhausted). If that is a realistic hope, then, because terrorism is generally able to limit killings, injuries and destruction of property by comparison with what happens in war, terrorism may sometimes be justifiable, even though it would be a form of self-deception to suggest that it is easier accurately to *anticipate* what will result from acts of terror than from acts of war.

It is highly unlikely, for instance, that the perpetrators of the attack on the World Trade Centre in New York (as distinct from that on the Pentagon) on 11 September 2001 anticipated not only how many deaths or injuries there would be and the impact of those deaths and injuries on the victims' families and friends, but the effect the attack would have on the economy of the United States, and, indeed, of the world as a whole; on the resolve of the United States to pursue their supporters; the effect that pursuit by the US military would have on the citizens of Afghanistan; the effect there would be on support for the grievances to which they were wishing to draw attention; and so on. I believe that the attack classically illustrates the claim that I have made that terrorism is a weapon of those who lack the power directly to attack those they oppose since, as far as the terrorists were concerned, the US mainland was invulnerable to a conventional military attack. That is why they aimed at targets symbolic of American hegemony in trade and commerce, and in military and political affairs. The point was to sting the United States, and that helps explain why there was no plan for a series of follow-up insurgencies (despite what the proponents of the so-called 'war on terrorism' would like us to believe). Of course, even if the perpetrators had had a crystal ball, and so been able to foresee all the effects of their actions, that would not have made it any easier morally to justify what they did, given the constraints against killing and injuring people, especially people engaged in innocent activities.

Until the world we live in becomes a fairer one for all concerned, it seems certain that those otherwise unable to have their serious and well-founded grievances remedied will sometimes resort to terrorism. Given that few instances of terrorism are likely to be morally justifiable (even among those involving only attacks on property, or on individuals who cannot be considered innocent), and, even more fundamentally, that it would be better not to have to resort to terrorism in any case, it must be part of our responsibility to work for the fairer world that would render terrorism unnecessary. We must not lose sight of the *jus ad bellum* whenever the requirements for *jus in bello* fail to be satisfied. So, for example, even if the manner of the terrorist attack on the World Trade Centre was unjustifiable, it is still necessary that the justice of the cause of those who carried out the attack be investigated (since their cause may be just despite the manner of their response). When supporters of the terrorists who died in the attack say that the attack was in response to the serious affront given to the Islamic world by the United States in propping up undemocratic and brutal regimes in the Middle East, including, but not only, Israel; in maintaining sanctions against Iraq despite the mounting toll on civilians, especially children; and in fostering US economic interests, even at the cost of impeding economic development within the predominantly Islamic nations, the United States ought to consider the justice of the complaints and, if appropriate, make amends. In that direction lies the best hope that terrorism of the kind unleashed on 11 September 2001 will be rendered unnecessary.

4

State Terrorism

Igor Primoratz

I

When it first entered political discourse, the word 'terrorism' was used with reference to the reign of terror imposed by the Jacobin regime—that is, to describe a case of state terrorism. Historians of the French Revolution have analysed and discussed that case in great detail. There are also quite a few historical studies of some other instances of state terrorism, most notably of the period of 'the Great Terror' in the Soviet Union.

In a contemporary setting, however, state terrorism is apparently much more difficult to discern. Discussions of terrorism in social sciences and philosophy tend to focus on non-state and, more often than not, anti-state terrorism. In common parlance and in the media, terrorism is as a rule assumed to be an activity of non-state agencies in virtue of the very meaning of the word. If one suggests that the army or security services are doing the same things that, when done by insurgents, are invariably described and condemned as terrorist, the usual reply is, 'But these are actions done on behalf of the state, in pursuit of legitimate state aims: the army, waging war, or the security services, fending off threats to our security.' In other words,

> *Throwing a bomb is bad,*
> *Dropping a bomb is good;*
> *Terror, no need to add,*
> *Depends on who's wearing the hood.*[1]

As far as everyday discourse and the media are concerned, this can perhaps be explained by two related tendencies. One is the widely shared assumption that, at least normally, what the state does has a certain kind of legitimacy, while those challenging it tend to be perceived as the forces of disorder and destruction, engaged in clearly unjustifiable pursuits. The other is the double standard of the form 'Us vs Them'. In states facing insurgency, the general public and the media find themselves on the side of the state. This tends to affect the usage. An offshoot of this tendency is that when insurgents abroad are sponsored by our state, we do not call them terrorists, but rather guerrillas, freedom fighters, and the like.

The focusing on non-state terrorism in social sciences is given a different explanation: that whatever the similarities between state and non-state terrorism, the dissimilarities are more prominent and instructive. Walter Laqueur, a leading authority on the history and sociology of terrorism, tells us that the two 'fulfil different functions and manifest themselves in different ways,' and that 'nothing is gained by ignoring the specifics of violence.'[2] I am not convinced that this approach is to be preferred in social science;[3] but be that as it may, it certainly will not do in moral philosophy. If some acts of state agencies are basically similar to and exhibit the same morally relevant traits as acts of non-state agencies commonly termed terrorist, that will clearly determine our moral understanding and evaluation of both. Thus philosophers have been less reluctant than sociologists and political scientists to recognise and discuss state terrorism.[4]

But the philosophical work on the subject done so far leaves room, and indeed suggests the need, for a typology of state involvement in terrorism, and a fuller statement of the argument for the claim philosophers sometimes make in passing that state terrorism is worse, morally speaking, than terrorism by non-state agencies. My aim in this paper is to offer some brief comments on these two topics. But first I need to say a few words on the definition of terrorism.

II

I have argued elsewhere that, for the purposes of philosophical discussion, terrorism is best defined as the deliberate use of violence, or threat of its use, against innocent people, with the aim of intimidating some other people into a course of action they otherwise would not take.[5]

Defined in this way, terrorism has two targets. One person or group is attacked directly, in order to get at another person or group and intimidate them into doing something they otherwise would not do. In terms of importance, the indirect target is primary, and the direct target secondary. The secondary, but directly attacked, target is innocent people. They are innocent in the sense of not having done anything the terrorist could cite as making them deserve the harm inflicted on them. According to the mainstream view of the morality of war, in an armed conflict, this includes all except members of armed forces and security services, those who supply them with arms and ammunition, and political officials directly involved in the conflict.[6] In this way we can distinguish between terrorism, on the one hand, and war and political violence, on the other. This is not to say that political violence cannot intimidate and coerce (it often does), nor that an army cannot employ terrorism (many armies have done so, and that, indeed, is one of the main types of state terrorism).

The definition acknowledges the historical connection of 'terrorism' with 'terror' and 'terrorising'. It does not confine terrorism to the political sphere, but makes it possible to speak of non-political (e.g. criminal) terrorism.

The definition is politically neutral: it covers both state and anti-state, revolutionary and counterrevolutionary, left-wing and right-wing terrorism. It is also morally neutral at the fundamental level of debate. I believe it captures the elements of terrorism that lead most of us to judge it as gravely wrong: the use or threat of use of *violence* against the *innocent* for the sake of *intimidation* and *coercion*. But it does not prejudge the moral question of its justification in particular cases. For it entails only that terrorism is *prima facie* wrong, and thus does not rule out its justification under certain circumstances.

Another virtue of the definition is that it relates the issue of the moral standing of terrorism to just war theory. For the central tenet of that theory, under the heading of *jus in bello*, is that we must not deliberately attack the innocent.

Clearly, the definition is both narrower in some respects and wider in others than the common usage would warrant. Attacks of insurgents on soldiers or police officers, which the authorities and the media depict, and the public perceives, as terrorist, would not count as such, but rather as political violence or guerrilla warfare. The bombing of German and Japanese cities in World War II, or numerous Israeli Army attacks on Lebanon, on the other hand, are commonly presented as acts of war, but would count as terrorism on my definition.

If it is said that this tells against the definition, my reply is that it need not. My point is that, if what we hope for is more discerning and critical moral understanding of these matters, we should not be unduly bound by conventional usage. What matters is that in the former case, the targets are soldiers or police officers, and not innocent people. In the latter case, innocent people are deliberately targeted with the aim of intimidation and coercion. The former case does not involve the four morally problematic components the definition singles out; the latter does. On the other hand, whether the bomb is planted by hand or dropped from an aircraft, and who does or does not wear the hood, can hardly matter, morally speaking.

III

Philosophers tend to be perceived as given to introducing all manner of distinctions where none were acknowledged before. With respect to state terrorism this has been the case to a lesser degree than on most other issues. Thus Alan Ryan discusses the claim that 'a terrorist state' is logically impossible by virtue of the definition of 'state', and brings up Nazi Germany and Stalin's Soviet Union as obvious counterexamples. Further on he writes: 'If Syria paid for, protected, equipped, and assisted hijackers and would-be bombers of El Al aircraft, that makes the Syrian regime a terrorist regime'.[7] This looks rather like a leaf from the US State Department's book; for the purpose of moral assessment, it is clearly much too rough. However repugnant Syria's sponsorship of Palestinian terrorism may have been, it is certainly not in the same moral league with the regimes of Hitler and Stalin. Surely we ought to differentiate more carefully.

When speaking of state involvement in terrorism, there are distinctions to be made both in terms of degree of such involvement and with regard to its victims.

Concerning the degree of state involvement in terrorism, we should withstand the temptation to classify every state that has made use of terrorism, either directly or by proxy, as a *terrorist state*. I suggest that we reserve this label for states that do not merely resort to terrorism on certain occasions and for certain purposes, but employ it in a lasting and systematic way, and indeed are defined, in part, by the sustained use of terrorism against their own population. These are *totalitarian states*, such as Nazi Germany, the Soviet Union in Stalin's time, or Cambodia under the rule of the Khmer Rouge.

A totalitarian regime aims at total domination of society and total unanimity of its subjects. Such an aim can only be pursued by an appropriately radical means: incessant terrorism, inflicted by an omnipresent and omnipotent secret police on an atomised and utterly defenceless population. Its efficiency is due, for the most part, to its arbitrary character: to the unpredictability of its choice of victims. Students of totalitarianism have pointed out that both in the Soviet Union and in Nazi Germany the regime at first brutally suppressed all its opponents; when it no longer had any opposition to speak of, it deployed its secret police against 'potential opponents'. In the Soviet Union it was eventually unleashed on masses of victims chosen at random. In the words of Carl J. Friedrich and Zbigniew K. Brzezinski, totalitarian terrorism

> aims to fill everyone with fear and vents in full its passion for unanimity. Terror then embraces the entire society ... Indeed, to many it seems as if they are hunted, even though the secret police may not touch them for years, if at all. Total fear reigns ... The total scope and the pervasive and sustained character of totalitarian terror are operationally important. By operating with the latest technological devices, by allowing no refuge from its reach, and by penetrating even the innermost sanctums of the regime ... it achieves a scope unprecedented in history. The atmosphere of fear it creates easily exaggerates the strength of the regime and helps it achieve and maintain its façade of unanimity. Scattered opponents of the regime, if still undetected, become isolated and feel themselves cast out of society. This sense of loneliness, which is the fate of all but more especially of an opponent of the totalitarian regime, tends to paralyse resistance ... It generates the universal longing to 'escape' into the anonymity of the collective whole.[8]

While only totalitarian states use terrorism in this way and with such an aim, many states that are clearly not totalitarian, including many basically democratic and liberal states, have used terrorism on a much more limited scale and for more specific purposes. They have done so directly, or by sponsoring non-state agencies whose *modus operandi* is, or includes, terrorism. But as their resort to terrorism is occasional rather than sustained, let alone essential, they should not be termed terrorist states. When they are, an important moral, political, and legal divide is blurred.

Another distinction is that between the use of terrorism by a state *against its own citizens*, and the use of terrorism *abroad*, as a means of foreign policy, war, or occupation. Other things being equal, state terrorism of the former type seems worse, morally speaking, than that of the latter type. For in the former case the state is attacking the very population for which it should be providing order, security, and justice.

Quite a few non-totalitarian states have made use of terrorism against their own population. Some have done so directly, by having state agencies such as the armed forces or security services employ terrorism. Many military dictatorships in South America and elsewhere are examples of this; the most extreme cases are, of course, Chile under Augusto Pinochet and Argentina under the generals. Other states have done the same indirectly, by sponsoring death squads and the like.

Many states, both totalitarian and non-totalitarian, have used terrorism abroad as a means of achieving foreign policy objectives, in the course of waging war, or as a method of maintaining their occupation of another people's land.

These types of state involvement in terrorism are not mutually exclusive; indeed, they are often complementary. A terrorist state will see no moral reason for hesitating to use terrorism beyond its borders too, whether in the course of waging war or in peacetime, as a means of pursuing its foreign policy objectives. Both Nazi Germany and the Soviet Union provide examples of that. But the same is true of states that do not qualify as terrorist, but do resort to terrorism against their own population on certain occasions and for some specific purposes. Such states, too, are not likely to be prevented by moral scruples from using terrorism abroad as well, whether directly or by proxy, when that is found expedient.

On the other hand, the fact that a state has resorted to terrorism in the international arena need not make it more prone to do the same at home, as there is a fairly clear line between the two. But it might. Since its establishment, Israel has often made use of terrorism in its conflict with the Palestinians and neighbouring Arab states. The suppression of the second Palestinian uprising (*intifada*) that is taking place at the time of writing is carried out, in part, by state terrorism. (Israel's neighbours, on their part, have supported

Palestinian terrorism against Israel.) The way Israeli police put down the demonstrations of Palestinians living in Israel proper, as its citizens, in October 2000—by shooting at them with rubber-coated and live ammunition and killing thirteen—may well qualify as state terrorism. If it does, that shows how the willingness to resort to terrorism abroad can eventually encourage its use at home.

To be sure, in practice the dichotomy of state and non-state terrorism does not always apply. Attempts at drawing hard and fast lines cannot succeed because of the widespread phenomenon of terrorist organisations receiving various types and degrees of support by states. Since in such cases a simple division of terrorism into state and non-state is no longer feasible, the moral assessment too becomes much more complex.

IV

All terrorism is extremely morally wrong. But not everything that is extremely morally wrong is wrong in the same degree. State terrorism can be said to be morally worse than terrorism by non-state agencies for at least four reasons.

First, although unwilling to extend the scope of his discussion of terrorism to include state terrorism, Walter Laqueur notes that 'acts of terror carried out by police states and tyrannical governments, in general, have been responsible for a thousand times more victims and more misery than all actions of individual terrorism taken together.'[9] He could also have mentioned terrorism employed by democracies (mostly, but not exclusively, in wartime), although that would not have affected the striking asymmetry very much. Now this asymmetry is not just another statistical fact; it follows from the nature of the state and the amount and variety of resources that even a small state has at its disposal. No matter how much non-state terrorists manage to enrich their equipment and improve their organisation, planning, and methods of action, they stand no chance of ever significantly changing the score. No insurgent, no matter how well funded, organised, determined, and experienced in the methods of terrorism, can hope to come close to the killing, maiming, and overall destruction on the scale the Royal Air Force (RAF) and US Air

Force visited on German and Japanese cities in World War II, or to the psychological devastation and subsequent physical liquidation of millions in Nazi and Soviet camps.

The terrorist attacks in the United States carried out on September 11 are in some respects rather unlike what we had come to expect from non-state terrorism. The number of victims, in particular, is unprecedented. Mostly because of that, I suspect, the media have highlighted these attacks as 'the worst case of terrorism ever'. So have quite a few 'public intellectuals'. Thus Salman Rushdie, in his monthly column in the *Age*, wrote of 'the most devastating terrorist attack in history'.[10] The number of people killed, believed to be approaching 7000 at the time, was indeed staggering. Yet 'the worst case of terrorism ever' mantra is but another instance of the tendency of the media to equate terrorism with non-state terrorism. When we discard the assumption that only insurgents engage in terrorism—as I submit we should—the overall picture changes significantly. Let me give just one example from the Allies' terror bombing campaign against Germany. In the night of 27 July 1943 the RAF carried out the second of its four raids on Hamburg, known as the 'Firestorm Raid'. In the morning, when both the attack itself and the gigantic firestorm it had created were over, some 40 000 civilians were dead.[11]

Second, in one way or another, state terrorism is bound to be compounded by secrecy, deception, and hypocrisy. When involved in terrorism—whether perpetrated by its own agencies or by proxy—a state will be acting clandestinely, disclaiming any involvement, and declaring its adherence to values and principles that rule it out. Or, if it is impractical and perhaps even counterproductive to deny involvement, it will do its best to present its actions to at least some audiences in a different light: as legitimate acts of war, or acts done in defence of state security. It will normally be able to do that without much difficulty, given the tendencies of common usage mentioned in Section I above.

Those engaging in non-state terrorism, on the other hand, need not be secretive, need not deceive the public about their involvement in terrorism (except, of course, at the operational level), and need not hypocritically proclaim their allegiance to moral principles that prohibit it. Some of them are amoralists, possibly of the sort exemplified by the notorious declaration of the nineteenth-century anarchist writer Laurent Tailhade: 'What do the victims matter if the gesture is beautiful!' Others exhibit what Aurel Kolnai has called 'overlain conscience':[12] conscience completely sub-jected to a non-moral absolute (the Leader, the Party, the Nation), which will permit and indeed enjoin all manner of actions incompatible with mainstream moral views, including terrorism. Still others adhere to some version of consequentialist moral theory, which will readily justify terrorism under appropriate circumstances.[13] In none of these cases will there be a need for deception and hypocrisy concerning the performance of specific terrorist acts or the adoption of policies of terrorism.

Third, virtually all actions that constitute terrorism are prohibited by one or another of the various international human rights declarations or conventions and agreements that make up the laws and customs of war. The latter provide for immunity of civilians in armed conflict and thus prohibit terrorism by belligerent sides. Most, if not all, remaining types of terrorism—terrorism in wartime perpetrated by groups not recognised as belligerent parties, and terrorism in time of peace perpetrated by anyone at all—are covered by the former. Now those engaging in non-state terrorism are not signatories to these declarations and conventions, while virtually all states today are signatories to most, if not all, of them. Therefore, when a state is involved in terrorism, it acts in violation of its own solemn international commitments. This particular charge cannot be brought against those resorting to non-state terrorism.

Fourth, non-state terrorism is often said to be justified, or at least that its wrongness is mitigated, by the argument of no alternative. In a case where, for instance, a people is subjected to foreign rule with the usual attendant evils of oppression, humiliation, and exploitation, which is utterly unyielding and deploys overwhelming power, a liberation movement may claim that the only effective method of struggle at its disposal is terrorism. To refrain from using terrorism in such circumstances would be tantamount to giving up the prospect of liberation altogether. Now this argument is often met with criticism. First, since terrorism is extremely morally wrong, the evils of foreign rule, grave as they may be, may not be enough to justify, or even mitigate, resort to it. After all, its victims would by definition be innocent people, rather than those responsible for these evils. Second, one can hardly ever be confident that terrorism will indeed achieve the aims adduced as its justification or mitigation. What people has ever succeeded in liberating itself by terrorism?

These objections are weighty, and may be enough to dispose of most attempts at justifying particular cases and policies of terrorism; but they do not show that the 'No alternative' argument will *never* work. Persecution and oppression of an ethnic, racial, or religious group can reach such an extreme point that even terrorism may properly be considered. And the question of its efficiency, being an empirical one, cannot be settled once and for all. So it is possible that a liberation movement should be facing such circumstances where resort to terrorism is indeed the only feasible alternative to the continuation of persecution and oppression so extreme as to amount to an intolerable moral disaster. In such a situation, the 'No alternative' argument would provide moral justification for terrorism, or at least somewhat mitigate our moral condemnation of its use. On the other hand, it seems virtually impossible that a state should find itself in such circumstances where it has no alternative to resorting to terrorism.

The only counterexample that comes to mind is the terror bombing campaign of the RAF against the civilian population of Germany in World War II, inasmuch as it can be seen as a case of 'supreme emergency' allowing one to set aside even an extremely grave moral prohibition in order to prevent an imminent moral catastrophe.[14] Yet even this example is of a very limited value. The supreme emergency argument may have been valid only during the first year of the campaign: in 1942 the victory of Nazi Germany in Europe—a major moral disaster by any standard—did appear imminent. However, after German defeats at El Alamein (6 November 1942) and at Stalingrad (2 February 1943), that was clearly no longer the case. But the campaign went on almost to the very end of the war. As Michael Walzer says, 'the truth is that the supreme emergency passed long before the British bombing reached its crescendo. The greater number by far of the German civilians killed by terror bombing were killed without moral (and probably also without military) reason.'[15]

My argument might be challenged by pointing out that what I have called terrorist regimes can maintain themselves only by employing sustained, large-scale terrorism against their own population. Furthermore, a state that would not qualify as terrorist in this sense may be waging a war whose aims can be achieved only by means of terrorism. The successive Serbian onslaughts on Croatia, Bosnia-Herzegovina, and Kosova in the 1990s are a clear example. Their aim was conquest, 'ethnic cleansing', and annexation of territories whose inhabitants included a non-Serb majority or large minority. Under the circumstances, and given the constraints of time, the 'cleansing' had to be accomplished by large-scale terrorism. The Serbs had no alternative.[16]

All this is true, but not to the point. In such cases terrorism is indeed the only efficient option and, if the aim is to be achieved, there is no alternative to its use. But in such cases, unlike at least some conceivable cases of non-state terrorism justified or mitigated by the 'No alternative' argument, the aim itself—the continuation of a Nazi or Stalinist regime, or the setting up of a greatly expanded and 'ethnically homogeneous' Serbia—can justify or mitigate nothing. Its achievement, rather than failure to achieve it, would amount to an intolerable moral disaster.

Another objection would refer to the 'balance of terror' produced by the mutual threat of nuclear attack that marked the Cold War period. The type of such threat relevant here was the threat of attacking the other side's civilian population centres. (In Cold War jargon, this was known as 'countervalue deterrence'.) If that threat was morally justified, it was a case of state terrorism justified by the 'No alternative' argument.

I am not convinced that it was justified. Clearly, carrying out the threat and actually destroying major population centres of the enemy and killing hundreds of thousands, if not millions, of enemy civilians, could never be morally justified. But does that mean that a threat to do so—made with the aim of preventing the chain of events that would make such destruction a serious option—is also morally impermissible? A positive reply to this question assumes that, if it is wrong to do X, it is also wrong to intend to do X, and therefore also to threaten to do X. This assumption has been questioned.[17] I have not made up my mind on this matter. One might try to circumvent the problem by arguing that the threat need not involve the intention of ever carrying it out; a bluff will do. Yet one might well wonder if a threat of this sort can be both credible and a bluff; and, of course, if the threat is not credible, it will not be morally justified either.

But this is too large a subject to go into in this paper. Therefore I will only say, in conclusion, that even if the 'balance of terror' generated by the threat of use of nuclear weapons against civilian targets turned out to be a convincing counterexample to my fourth argument for the claim that state terrorism is morally worse than terrorism employed by non-state agencies, the first three arguments would still stand and, I trust, suffice.[18]

5

Osama bin Laden, Terrorism and Collective Responsibility

Seumas Miller

Osama bin Laden and terrorism

Evidently, most of the world's people view the September 11 terrorist attacks on the World Trade Centre in New York and on the Pentagon in Washington DC as morally unjustified, indeed morally despicable. Perhaps a significant number of Muslims, while not condoning the attacks, nevertheless have some sympathy for the aims, if not the methods, of the attackers. Others might condemn the attacks, while also taking the view that the United States somehow brought it on themselves, or at least contributed to it, by their policies in supporting Israel against Palestine, in propping up autocratic Arab regimes, such as the Saudi regime to protect their oil and other interests, and by their large-scale covert CIA funding of extremist fundamentalist groups in Afghanistan via the Inter Services Intelligence agency (ISI), the Pakistani secret service, during the Soviet occupation of Afghanistan in the 1980s.[1] And doubtless many people in the so-called Third World are too preoccupied with threats to their own lives from violence and poverty to generate enormous amounts of sympathy for the victims of the September 11 attacks. As the journalist, George Alagiah, points out, in drawing the contrast between the reluctant and ineffectual international reaction to the genocide in Rwanda with the decisive and overwhelming response to the September 11 attacks, 'even in death the rich and the poor worlds are divided'.[2]

Given that the victims of these terrorist attacks were innocent people going about their daily business, the moral outrage that the attacks generated was understandable. On the other hand, given the unpopularity of the United States in many quarters of the

Arab world, it was predictable that in many Arab and other Islamic countries there would be mixed feelings; sympathy for the victims, but also a feeling that now finally the United States might understand what it means to be terrorised by people that you cannot reason with.[3]

These widely held, yet differing views, agree on one very important thing: the terrorist attacks were not morally justified. By contrast, there is a significant, albeit small, minority of the world's people who evidently believe that the September 11 attacks were, in fact, morally justified; indeed, not only justified but morally required. Here I have in mind members and supporters of extremist Islamist groups that advocate jihad or holy war against the United States and its allies.[4]

This extremist view appears to deny morality. The attacks deny morality since they were *terrorist* attacks, as opposed to attacks undertaken as a legitimate part of an otherwise just war, or for that matter an otherwise unjust war. Is not terrorism, by definition, morally unacceptable? Listening to George W. Bush and Tony Blair, and most of the world media, one certainly gets the impression that terrorism is both easily identifiable and, by definition, morally unacceptable.

In fact, the definition of terrorism is problematic, and terrorism takes a number of not necessarily mutually exclusive forms; for example, the state terrorism of Saddam Hussein or Augusto Pinochet, the anti-state terrorism of Hamas or the IRA, and the state-sponsored terrorism of extremist Muslim groups by Mummamar Gaddaffi or of extremist right-wing groups by the United States in Latin America.[5]

Note here that Osama bin Laden's al-Qaeda might be referred to as a species of non-state terrorism directed principally at non-Muslim Western states, especially the United States, that are alleged to be attacking Islam. While Osama bin Laden and al-Qaeda found a natural home and ally among the fundamentalist Islamist Taliban in Afghanistan, his organisation is global in character. For Osama bin Laden had put together a loose coalition of extremist Islamist groups based in a variety of locations, including Egypt, Algeria, Afghanistan, Sudan and Pakistan. Peter Bergen refers to it as 'Holy War Inc.'[7]

It is important to note, however, that the brand of Islam propounded by Osama bin Laden has little in common with the more moderate forms of Islam to be found throughout the Muslim world in places such as Indonesia, India and, for that matter, the Middle East and North Africa. For example, Osama bin Laden is anti-democratic, opposed to the emancipation of women, and opposed to the modern secular state with its division between religious institutions and the state. So Osama bin Laden is opposed to more secular Muslim governments such as those in Egypt, and even Iraq. And he is implacably opposed to pro-Western Muslim governments such as Saudi Arabia, no matter how religiously conservative they are. Given all this, the prospects of Osama bin Laden and his followers setting up a sustainable long-term Islamic state, let alone an Islamic empire of the kind his pronouncements hearken back to, are not good. If he is still alive, his role in all probability will remain that of a terrorist; a force for destabilisation only.

Moreover, the fact that al Qaeda is opposed to democracy and the emancipation of women ensures that it does not have moral legitimacy; if recent world history has taught any moral lessons at all, the moral unacceptability of autocracy and of the suppression of women are surely among them.

So, some of its main goals are morally objectionable. What of its methods?

The preparedness of Osama bin Laden's followers to commit suicide, and thereby supposedly achieve martyrdom, is an enormous advantage for a terrorist organisation. Moreover, this role is greatly facilitated not only by real and perceived injustices, and already existing national, ethnic and religious conflict, but also by global financial interdependence and modern technology, such as the global communication system and the new weapons of mass destruction that he has been seeking to develop. Perhaps al Qaeda's success is not dependent on widespread political and popular support for its goals, although it is certainly reliant on disaffection, including with US policies. Rather its success might largely be a function of the psychological preparedness and logistical capacity to perpetrate acts of terror, coupled with the technological capacity to communicate those acts, and thereby wreak havoc in a globally economically interdependent world. Its methods have proved extraordinarily effective in relation to the goal of destabilisation. The terrorist group from the medieval past has identified the Achilles' heel in the security systems of the modern civilised world.

For our purposes here, terrorism can be thought of as the intentional killing, maiming or otherwise harming, or threatening to harm, innocent people—or at least non-attackers—as a means of achieving political or military purposes. Here the notion of an innocent victim is problematic. However, there are a number of salient points. First, the notion of terrorism being used here is relativised to the specific conflict in question. So people are innocent if they are not opposing the terrorists by, for example, perpetrating any alleged wrongdoing the terrorists are seeking to redress, or trying to kill or apprehend the terrorists. Second, there are going to be clear cases of innocent victims, on any acceptable account of innocence, for instance children. Third, and perhaps most controversially, intentionally killing the so-called innocent is not necessarily morally unacceptable, and thus terrorism as defined here is not necessarily morally unacceptable. As Burleigh Taylor Wilkins notes, perhaps the Jews in Nazi Germany would have been morally justified in deploying terrorist strategies against ordinary Germans, if they could have, and if doing so would have averted the Holocaust.[8] More generally, there is an issue of the justification of terrorism as a tactic deployed as a response to terrorism, as opposed to using terror to redress injustice. Consider in this connection the tactics used against terrorists in the Punjab by the Indian police under the leadership of K. P. S. Gill in the 1980s.

The September 11 attacks were performed in the name of moral righteousness by people prepared to give up their own lives, as well as the lives of those that they murdered. Osama bin Laden himself may well have been principally driven by hatred and a desire for revenge, but he and likeminded religious extremists have managed to mobilise moral sentiment, indeed moral outrage, to their cause, and they have done so on a significant scale. In this respect they are, of course, not unique among terrorist groups. Terrorist groups typically come into existence because of, and are sustained by, some real or imagined injustice.

Moreover, in order for Osama bin Laden and his group to mobilise moral sentiment they have had to overcome, at least in the minds of their followers, what might be regarded as commonly held principles of moral acceptability, including the principle according to which only those responsible for injustice or harm should be targeted. Yet the majority of those killed, and intended to be killed by the September 11 terrorists, were—according to commonly held principles of moral responsibility—innocent victims. They included not only civilians, but also children, visiting foreign nationals, and so on. This being so, what possible moral justification could be offered by the terrorists and their supporters?

One justification does not necessarily overthrow commonly held principles of moral responsibility, rather it simply appeals to the principle that the ends justify the means. It is not that those who are killed by terrorists deserve to die; indeed their death may well be a matter of regret to the terrorists. However, killing these innocent people is the only way to further the righteous cause, and the moral importance of that cause overrides the evil that consists in killing some innocents; or so the argument goes. This argument assumes that the end in question is a very morally weighty one. As we have seen, al-Qaeda's goals, far from being morally weighty, are morally unacceptable. However, there are likely to be at least notional scenarios under which the ends will justify terrorism as a means. It is just a matter of circumscribing the extent of terror to be used, and then raising the stakes to the point where the end must be achieved. What if torturing or shooting dead a small number of innocent people was the only way to save an evil dictator from launching a nuclear strike and destroying the world?

Naturally, any particular recourse to terrorism may not realise the ends of the terrorists. Consider the failed terror tactics of the Red Brigade in the 1970s in Europe. As far as al-Qaeda's likelihood of realising its ultimate goals is concerned, as I have already indicated, the prospects are not good. Finally, even if terrorism does realise its ends, and they are good ends, it can still be maintained that the ends realised in some given situation do not justify the particular means used.

No doubt the idea that the ends justify the means is a line of reasoning that has considerable weight with terrorists in general, and with Osama bin Laden's al-Qaeda organisation, in particular. And doubtless there have been instances, such as in Algeria and Kenya during the French and British (respectively) colonial periods, where terrorism did achieve its ends, whether or not achieving these ends did justify the terrorist methods used. Perhaps in the case of Algeria it was a case in part of activists deploying terrorist tactics as a response to terror directed at themselves.

Certainly, Osama bin Laden needs to rely *in part* on the ends-justify-the-means argument. If the ultimate ends of terrorism are not good ends, then it is immoral. And, if terrorism does not realise its ends, then it seems both irrational and immoral. However, bin Laden himself did not seem to rely *exclusively* on the argument. For Osama bin Laden denied, at least implicitly, that so-called innocent victims of his terrorist attacks are, in fact, innocent. For example, on 22 February 1998 in announcing the formation of the World Islamic Front for Jihad against the Jews and the Crusaders he said:

> All those crimes and calamities are an explicit declaration by the Americans of war on Allah, His Prophet, and Muslims . . . Based upon this and in order to obey the Almighty, we hereby give Muslims the following judgment: The judgment to kill and fight Americans and their allies, whether civilians or military, is an obligation for every Muslim who is able to do so in any country.[9]

Accordingly, perhaps Osama bin Laden believes that his brand of terrorism is both likely to realise its ends, and that it is morally acceptable by virtue of the guilt of its victims; it is essentially self-defence against terrorism. Is there any real or alleged basis for this latter belief?

Evidently, the justification for denying the innocence of US civilians is collectivist in character. The idea seems to be that certain collectives, namely Islam and the United States (or perhaps Islam and Christianity or Islam and the Jews), and formerly Islam and Communist Russia in Afghanistan, are locked in struggle in the manner that two individual human agents might be.

Osama bin Laden and thousands of other Arab Muslims went to Afghanistan in the 1980s to join the Afghans in their fight against the godless communist invaders from Russia. According to Osama bin Laden, Islam won a great victory against the Russian superpower.

Osama bin Laden claimed that Islam was fighting the United States in order to defend itself against the threats to its existence posed by the United States. Such US actions as the ongoing support of Israel, the Somalian intervention, US military bases in Saudi Arabia (the country in which are located the two most holy Islamic sites, Mecca and Medina) and the sanctions against Iraq that have caused the death of hundreds of thousands of Iraqi— and therefore Muslim—children demonstrate the threat to Islam posed by the United States.

Moreover, allegedly this attack upon Islam is a longstanding one, and the attackers have simply refused to listen to reasoned argument, but have instead subjected Islam to the considerable weight of Western economic and military power. (Hence Osama bin Laden's choice in the September 11 attacks of symbols of that power, namely the World Trade Centre and the Pentagon.) Given this collectivist conception, all US citizens (and citizens of their allies) can be regarded as a collective threat to Islam, and as being collectively guilty for the ongoing attacks on Islam. Accordingly, so the logic seems to run, there can be nothing wrong in killing US citizens, irrespective of whether they are combatants, or otherwise intentionally supporting US military actions.

What are we to make of this justification of terrorism by recourse to collective moral responsibility? Osama bin Laden's pronouncements are objectionable on a number of counts. For one thing, his account and analysis of US actions and policies are simplistic and, in large part, fallacious. The US bases in Saudi Arabia are presumably there for the purpose of protecting the flow of oil, and to try to contain Saddam Hussein, rather than to undermine Islam.

Nor has the United States waged war against Islam as such; although Osama bin Laden sought to present its attacks on Iraq, and its attacks on the Taliban in Afghanistan, as war on Islam itself. And whatever the rights and wrongs of specific US policies against particular Muslim states and communities, including war against Iraq, the United States is not engaging in a terrorist campaign against Islam as such.

Moreover, the United States' alleged protagonist, namely Islam, seems far from the unitary agent referred to in Osama bin Laden's pronouncements. Consider the Iran/Iraq war, or the role of Pakistan in destabilising Afghanistan. On the other hand, the US support for Israel in its war with Palestine, and for autocratic regimes, such as the Saudi regime, that repress ordinary Arab and Islamic people, and various other US policies, such as the sanctions against Iraq, provide fertile ground for anti-US feeling in the Islamic world. Indeed, if the recent work of the well-known scholar Samuel Huntington is to be given any credence, Osama bin Laden's conception of a Western versus Islamic confrontation is not entirely without foundation. Huntington's view is essentially collectivist in character.[10] It is just that whereas Osama bin Laden seems to think Islam is the object of the threat, Huntington thinks it is the source.

For another thing, Osama bin Laden's pronouncements on the collective guilt of all Americans are facile, and evidently inconsistent with the Qur'an itself; for example, on the issue of killing non-combatants.

At any rate, in so regarding groups of individual human beings in this collectivist light, or lights, it is arguable that certain untoward consequences follow, or at least are facilitated. For one thing, terrorists, and military organisations more generally, can more easily justify the killing of innocents. For innocent victims are typically at least members of the collective, the state or ethnic or religious group or whatever, that is the object of the terrorists' anger. Accordingly, they can be killed as being members of, say, the US citizenry. Moreover, the value of the lives of these individual innocent victims can be given a discount, and in the limiting case of genocide, can be regarded as having no value. Consider the Holocaust or the Rwandan genocide.

Nor is this tendency restricted to terrorist organisations. Consider the My Lai massacre. Again, policies of pursuing military tactics that involve killing innocent victims rather than risking lives of one's own combatants seem to partake of this logic. Consider the atomic bombs dropped on Hiroshima and Nagasaki, or the recent tactic of bombing raids in Kosovo preferred by NATO to the tactic of deploying ground troops. Apparently, the life of one of one's own country's combatants is worth many times that of an innocent civilian who happens to be another country with whom one is at war, or indeed of another ethnic group one is supposedly protecting. This inconsistent view is implicit in the policy of continuing sanctions against Iraq, notwithstanding the fact that it was leading to the starvation and death of hundreds of thousands of Iraqi children, and was not preventing Saddam Hussein from continuing with his programme of developing a nuclear, chemical and biological weapons capability.

Collective responsibility

So much for the collectivist features and tendencies implicit in the pronouncements, policies and actions of terrorists, such as Osama bin Laden, and to a much lesser extent in that of their protagonists, such as the United States. What we now need to do is directly address the philosophical issue of collective responsibility and terrorism. Under what conditions, if any, can a group of so-called victims of terrorism be regarded as guilty by virtue of their collective responsibility for the injustices that the terrorists in question are seeking to redress?

As it happens, there are a number of philosophical theories of collective responsibility that might be deployed to justify some acts of terrorism, though presumably not those perpetrated by Osama bin Laden and his followers. These include the collectivist—as opposed to individualist—theories of David Cooper[11] and Peter French.[12] A more moderate collectivist theoretical account, and one that explicitly addresses the issue of terrorism, is that offered by Burleigh Taylor Wilkins.[13]

By contrast with individualist conceptions of collective responsibility for action, collectivists offer accounts according to which individuals, especially members of national, ethnic and religious groups, can be held responsible for the actions of those groups, even where the individuals in question did not contribute to those actions. Thus David Cooper holds that some collective entity can be morally responsible for some outcome, even though no individual member of that entity was even partly morally responsible. Peter French also holds this view. Moreover, these theorists maintain that such collective entities are moral agents, and therefore can be legitimately praised and blamed, rewarded and punished.

I have argued against these collectivist conceptions elsewhere.[14] Here I simply note that in the context of conflictual situations, such as war and terrorism, these collectivist theories bring with them a significant problem. Unless we are to assume that collective agents are purely epiphenomenal entities that can be punished or rewarded without any causal effect on their individual members—a view French explicitly rejects—then the way is clear to harm individuals for wrongs that they did not contribute to, so long as those individuals are members of collective entities that have done wrong. This goes a long way to providing a theoretical justification for al-Qaeda's terrorist attacks of September 11. For if we assume that the US government policies in relation to Israel, Saudi Arabia and so on, are morally unacceptable, then the way is evidently clear to kill US citizens in the name of retaliating against the unacceptable US policies.

The consequences of such collectivist accounts are very unpalatable indeed. For these and other reasons, these forms of collectivism ought to be rejected. Moreover, there are other theoretical or quasi-theoretical views that are similarly unacceptable. One such view rests on the claim of inter-relatedness. If we take harm as including both direct and indirect harm, then, for example, a US citizen who paid taxes that were used to train a pilot who bombed a Taliban stronghold might be held to be responsible for the deaths of the civilians killed. Clearly, moral responsibility

cannot be ascribed merely on the basis of possibly very indirect, and entirely unforeseen, causal contributions. This view is as unpalatable as the one ascribing moral responsibility on the basis of membership of the group.

An alternative conception to these somewhat farfetched views has been provided by Burleigh Taylor Wilkins. Wilkins is an individualist, who nevertheless believes that in some instances terrorism can be morally justified, and justified in part on the basis of group membership.

Roughly speaking, Wilkins's idea is that the members of a group can be held strictly liable for the policies of the group in an analogous manner to that in which employers can be held liable for the actions of their employees, notwithstanding the fact that the employers did not contribute to these actions of their employees.

I have two fundamental problems with Wilkins's view. First, employers and their employees are functioning in a highly structured and legally regulated organisational setting in which, in effect, they undertake vicarious and strict liability in relation to a specified range of their employees' actions. This is not analogous to being a member of an ethnic or religious or even national group.

Second, the actions for which an employee might be vicariously strictly liable would not typically include massive rights violations on the part of their employees; what employer would agree to be held liable for these? Moreover, the nature or extent of liability would not typically include giving up one's life.

I conclude that Wilkins has not made out the case for strict liability in the very different context of war and terrorism, and in any case his account is far too permissive.

Is there a less-permissive modified form of individualism that might offer a justification for at least some forms of terrorism, namely forms in which the victims of terror, while not attackers, nevertheless are in some sense collectively morally responsible for rights violations? I believe that there is, and the collective responsibility as joint responsibility account that I have developed elsewhere, provides a starting point for this account.[15]

On this view individuals who perform a joint action are collectively, or jointly, responsible for the goals realised by that action. But what is a joint action?[16]

Roughly speaking, two or more individuals perform a joint action if each of them intentionally performs an individual action, but does so in the true belief that in so doing they will jointly realise an end that each of them has. Having an end in this sense is a mental state in the head of one or more individuals, but it is neither a desire not an intention. However, it is an end that is not realised by one individual acting alone. So we have called such ends, collective ends. For example, the terrorists who hijacked American Airlines Flight 11, and crashed the plane into the North Tower of the World Trade Centre in New York, performed a joint action. At least one terrorist operated the controls of the plane, while another navigated, and the remaining terrorists, by violence and the threat of violence, prevented the cabin crew and passengers from intervening. Each performed a contributory action, or actions, in the service of the collective end of crashing the plane into the building and killing passengers, office workers and themselves.

Here each agent is individually responsible for performing his contributory action, and responsible by virtue of the fact that he intentionally performed this action, and the action was not intentionally performed by anyone else. Of course, the other agents (or agent) *believe* that he is performing, or is going to perform, the contributory action in question. But mere possession of such a belief is not sufficient for the ascription of responsibility to *the believer* for performing the individual action in question. So what are the agents *collectively* responsible for? The agents are collectively responsible for the realisation of the (collective) *end* that results from their contributory actions.

In relation to some terrorism cause, it is evident that 'innocent' victims have not intentionally performed any relevant untoward individual action, and nor have they contributed to a joint action. Now there might be lesser roles that they have played, such as intentionally assisting such individual or joint actions, or unknowingly causally contributing to them. If so, they might have some form of significantly diminished responsibility. However, this line of reasoning is unlikely to yield an adequate in principle justification for terrorist attacks on innocent victims. For if the victims are essentially innocent, then there will be no justification, and if there is a justification then it will turn out that the victims are not after all innocent, or at least not wholly innocent. In some of these cases involving victims who have a measure of responsibility, terrorism might be justified, given the presence of very weighty consequentialist considerations. But in general it is hard to see how intentional killing of the sort practised by terrorists could be a morally justified response in the case of people who have at most a slight degree of moral responsibility for the injustices the terrorists are seeking to redress. Here I have in mind cases such as that of a US civilian killed in the September 11 attack who happened to vote for the Clinton and Bush administrations in the knowledge that they would ensure that sanctions would be applied to Iraq with the consequence—given Saddam Hussein's intransigence and lack of concern for his own people—that thousands of children would die of starvation.

Perhaps what is called for is a shift in emphasis from viewing the so-called innocent victims of the terrorist attacks as perpetrators of the injustices the terrorists are seeking to address, or assistants of the perpetrators, to viewing them as bystanders who ought to intervene. In other words, the innocent victims are at the level of action in large part innocent; however, at the level of inaction, they are not, they are guilty of sins of omission.

I say 'in large part' because it may well be that while someone is essentially a bystander who has a responsibility to intervene in relation to some wrong being done, they might be further implicated by unknowingly making an indirect causal contribution to that wrongdoing. Here I have in mind the kind of case in which (say) a US citizen votes for George W. Bush because he believes Bush will enact policies that will benefit the citizen economically, not because Bush will pursue policies that prop up autocratic regimes. Bush then pursues policies that prop up autocratic regimes that repress their citizens.

There are two general reasons that a bystander might be considered to be guilty of an act of omission. First, the wrong being done is of such a magnitude that someone ought to intervene, and as a bystander they are in a position to see what is going on, and to intervene. Second, they are not mere bystanders, but bystanders who are in effect benefiting from the wrong that is being done. Perhaps the US economy, and therefore US citizens, are benefiting from US government policy of propping up autocratic regimes in the Middle East, such as Saudi Arabia, in order to ensure the requisite continuing flow of reasonably cheap oil.

The fact that someone is benefiting from some wrongdoing, while not causally contributing to it, is not sufficient to ascribe to them any responsibility for that wrongdoing. So let us set this consideration aside and focus exclusively on omissions.[17]

Consider the case of a drowning man who could easily be saved by one or other of three bystanders. One of the bystanders simply needs to throw the drowning man a lifejacket; however, each refuses to do so. But the drowning man has a gun, and threatens to shoot one of the bystanders if either the bystander or one of his friends does not throw the jacket. They call his bluff, and the drowning man shoots one of the bystanders dead. In fear of his life, the next bystander then throws the jacket.

Intuitively, the drowning man's action seems morally justified, given his action was the only way to preserve this life. He had a positive right to be assisted, and the bystander was refraining from carrying out his duty to respect that right. So the case is analogous to those involving negative rights, such as the right not to be killed, or the right not to have one's freedom interfered with.

So in principle deadly force can be used to enforce positive rights, including presumably rights to subsistence, as well as to enforce negative rights.

Moreover, as is the case with negative rights, third parties—at least in principle—have rights, and indeed duties, to use deadly force to ensure that positive rights are respected.

This point presumably has implications for governments who intentionally refrain from respecting the positive rights, including subsistence rights, of their citizens. Consider Saddam Hussein's refusal to distribute much-needed food and medicine to his own citizens, albeit in the context of UN-sponsored sanctions. The citizens, or third parties, are entitled to use deadly force against these governments. Perhaps such use of deadly force, including assassination, is to be regarded as terrorism on the grounds that the victims of terrorism are not themselves attackers. If so, then terrorism can be morally justified in some circumstances. However, the victims in this kind of scenario are not innocent; their intentional acts of omission constitute violations of the positive rights of their citizens.

Some of these rights or duties to use deadly force to enforce positive rights might be exercised against certain categories of people with diminished responsibility. In the above example, suppose that the rescue takes place at sea and that one of the bystanders is the captain of a ship, and the others are crew members. Suppose further that the reason that the crew member is refusing to save the drowning man was that he was instructed not to assist him by his captain, and if he refused to obey it would be at some considerable cost to himself (he would be imprisoned). (Assume also that the drowning man is not in a position to shoot the captain, since he is at too great a distance.) Accordingly, the crew member seems to have diminished responsibility for failing to respect the drowning man's right to be rescued. Nevertheless, the drowning man is still entitled to shoot the crew member dead in order to preserve his own life.

By analogy, government employees, such as administrators or police who intentionally refrain from assisting those in need because instructed to do so by their government, might well be legitimate targets of 'terrorists'. Consider blacks in apartheid South Africa who were forcibly removed into desolate 'homelands', such as Qua Qua, and once there found they could not provide themselves with a basic subsistence. Now suppose South African politicians declare such 'homelands' to be Independent States—as in fact happened—and thereby try to absolve themselves of responsibility for the well-being of the 'citizens' of these alleged new states. Government officials who formulated these policies, administrators who implemented them, and police who enforced them, were all legitimate targets, on the assumption that killing these officials was necessary in order to ensure that the subsistence rights of these people would be realised. If this is terrorism, then it is justified terrorism. However, once again, the victims of such terror while they have diminished moral responsibility, are by no means entirely innocent.

In the case of members of a group or community we need to focus on the collective role of bystanders. So the members of the group or community are said to be collectively morally responsible for a collective omission. But here we need some theoretical account of collective responsibility for omissions. Elsewhere I have elaborated such an account.[18]

According to that account, members of some group are collectively responsible for failing to intervene to halt or prevent some serious wrongdoing or wrongful state of affairs if: (1) the wrongdoing took place, or is taking place; (2) the members of the community intentionally refrained from intervening; (3) each or most of the members intervening having as an end the prevention of the wrongdoing probably would have prevented, or have a reasonable chance of halting, the wrongdoing; (4) each of the members of the community would have intentionally refrained from intervening—and intervening having as an end the prevention or termination of the wrongdoing—even if the others, or most of the others, had intervened with that end in mind. Note that on this account, if an agent would have intervened, but done so only because the others did (that is, not because he had as an end the prevention or termination of the wrong), then the agent would still be morally responsible, jointly with the others, for failing to intervene—given conditions (1) to (3).

In the light of this definition, it might well be that South African officials who were in a position to assist destitute blacks in the 'homelands', members of the UN who failed to intervene militarily to assist Tutsi victims of the Rwanda genocide, and so on, are collectively responsible for omissions of a kind that might justify the use of deadly force to ensure that the rights to assistance in question are realised. If such recourse to deadly force is terrorism, it may well be justified terrorism. However, the victims of such terrorism are far from being innocent victims.

6

Towards Liberation: Terrorism from a Liberation Ideology Perspective

Aleksandar Pavković

Why liberation ideologies?

Liberation ideologies are a set of political beliefs, value judgements and exhortations to action that call for and justify the liberation of a group of oppressed people from oppression and their oppressors. I shall examine only one kind of liberation ideology, one that would consider any act of violence against the oppressors justified, provided—and this is an important proviso—that this act does indeed contribute to the liberation of the oppressed. This excludes liberation ideologies that do not justify violence against oppressors, or justify violence only against particular agents of oppression.

For the purposes of the present chapter, it is assumed that some forms of terrorism involve using violence against persons who in their everyday occupation do not coerce anyone, or do not help anyone to do so (or who are not capable of doing so). As Robert Young points out in his essay in this volume, this is not the only kind of violence that terrorists use and, therefore, this kind of violence cannot (or should not) be used to define terrorism.[1] However, justifications of terrorism to be discussed in this essay concern the use of terrorist violence of this very kind; for this reason I shall restrict my discussion to terrorist violence of this kind alone.

In this chapter I examine the justifications of terrorism advanced by the anti-colonialist activist and writer, Dr Frantz Fanon, in his essay 'Concerning Violence' published in 1961,[2] and by Osama bin Laden, the leader of the Islamic al-Qaeda group, in his messages broadcast in 2001. I shall first outline the two justifications of terrorist violence, and then consider how Fanon and his supporter Jean-Paul Sartre defend their justification of terrorism against those objections arising from a familiar ethical view that I shall call universal humanism. The essay will point out the differences in ethical principles and values between an ideology of liberation of the violent kind and the latter view that condemns violence against non-threatening and unarmed civilians.

In order to understand Fanon's justification of the use of violence and of terrorism, it is necessary to examine the key concepts of his ideology: that of the oppressed, of the oppression and of the liberation. As we shall see, in his justification of terrorist violence perpetrated by his followers, Osama bin Laden used quite similar concepts. Fanon's essay has been translated into Persian by the influential Islamic thinker Ali Shariati. While his ideology originates in a religious worldview quite different from (and often incompatible with) Fanon's Marxist worldview, the similarity between the key concepts they use is quite striking; for this reason a discussion of Fanon's theoretical framework may be of some help in understanding Osama bin Laden's justification of terrorism.

The oppressed versus the oppressors: Key concepts of an ideology of liberation

The *oppressed* were, in the context of Fanon's writing, usually colonised peoples, defined by their race—non-European—and by their status of being colonised or controlled by another race, the Europeans. But the oppressed could also be defined not only by their race but also by their class, their profession or the lack of it, their nationality and, of course, their religion. However defined, the oppressed group is in some tangible sense politically unequal to another group that exerts a degree of unwanted or undesirable control over them, and in doing so humiliates or denigrates them. According to Fanon, in a system of oppression the oppressors believe that the oppressed are neither culturally nor cognitively equal to them, and therefore deserve to be controlled and oppressed; they justify their oppression by the latter's inferiority. Thus the oppressed are humiliated not only because they are controlled but because in being controlled they are presented as incapable of the autonomy characteristic of other human beings. This strips them of their human dignity. Even if the extent of control over members of the oppressed group is varied, the humiliation inflicted on all members of the group is equal: they are all considered more or less inferior to the oppressors.

The *oppressors* are the controllers—those who possess the means of control and who participate in controlling the oppressed. In Fanon's writings they are defined again by their race—the Europeans—and their social and political role—that of colonisers. But the oppressors could also be defined by their profession, class, nationality or religion and not only by their race. In fact, the oppressors are not only those who in effect do the controlling— say, government officials, corporation employees or bosses—but any member of the group who in any way participates in the system of oppression. Thus, if the French are the oppressors of the native population of Algiers (as Fanon sees them in his writings), any French person involved in any way in the system of oppression belongs to the group of oppressors. 'Being involved in the system of oppression' is, intentionally, a very broad and rather undefined category. Such a wide and collective definition of the oppressors was clearly needed to establish a parallel with the previous definition of the oppressed: each member of the oppressed group (for example, a colonised people) is subject to oppression and, by analogy, each member of the oppressor group shares in the oppression. Within the framework of this ideology, a person is an oppressor not in virtue of any specific act of oppression but in virtue of belonging to the group that collectively does the oppressing. This type of collective definition of the oppressors by analogy with the group of oppressed ensures that, within this framework, there are no 'innocents' among the oppressors as there are no 'non-oppressed' among the oppressed.

According to Fanon, in paradigmatic cases of oppression, those of colonised peoples, oppression involves the use of physical violence against the oppressed, although not necessarily against all, or even the majority of them. Apart from targeting those who oppose them, colonisers often use violence in a random and arbitrary way against any member of the oppressed group so as to assert their authority and to spread fear and terror.

Osama bin Laden's October 2001 message suggests that, like Fanon, he believed that the violence suffered by the oppressed and their ensuing humiliation justifies their acts of terrorist violence against their (alleged) oppressors:

Our nation (the Islamic world) has been tasting this humiliation and this degradation for more than 80 years. Its sons are killed, its blood is shed, its sanctuaries are attacked, and no one hears and no one heeds. When God blessed one of the groups of Islam, vanguards of Islam, they destroyed America. I pray to God to elevate their status and bless them. Millions of innocent children are being killed as I speak . . . When the sword comes down (on America), after 80 years, hypocrisy rears its ugly head. They deplore and they lament for those killers, who have abused the blood, honour and sanctuaries of Muslims. The least that can be said about those people is that they are debauched. They have followed injustice. They supported the butcher over the victim, the oppressor over the innocent child . . . The winds of change have come to eradicate oppression from the island of Muhammad, peace be upon him.[3]

According to Osama bin Laden, the oppressed and their oppressors are each defined by their religion: the oppressed are the Muslims or the Islamic nation and the oppressors are non-Muslim or infidel. The former have been exposed to indiscriminate killing, including that of children, to disrespect of their religion and its sanctuaries, and, as a result of this, to a continuous humiliation and degradation. The oppressors have either committed these hostile and unjust acts against the Muslims or, in some undefined sense, have supported them. This makes them morally depraved or morally inferior to the oppressed. All this, Osama bin Laden believed, justifies violent revenge or retribution against the oppressors. Whether a construction of the two opposed groups and of their mutual relations in this way has any truth value or not, is a question that is further explored by Seamus Miller and others in this collection; in this chapter I shall only consider the role this kind of distinction plays in a justification of terrorist violence.

Liberation from oppression

According to Fanon, it is the superior technology and superior command over the instruments of oppression that enable oppressors to control, at least temporarily, the oppressed. In paradigmatic cases, the oppressors possessed superior military hardware—for example, guns—as well as much more efficient military and state organisation than the oppressed. The oppressed, therefore, cannot compete with them on the level of technological and military organisation. However, the oppressor's use of violence, Fanon suggests, is subject to some constraint both from inside and outside their own (oppressors') community. First, the oppressors are constrained by the cost of their oppression and their use of violence; if this is resisted, the cost of overcoming resistance may be greater to them than the benefits to be gained from the use of violence or from the oppression itself. Second, they are constrained by domestic public opinion and by public opinion in other states that do not participate in that oppression. In the post-1945 era public opinion in West European and North American states has grown rather squeamish when confronted with the media reports of large-scale violence against civilians; at least in some cases this appears to have constrained the deployment of such violence. How significant or effective such a constraint is, is subject to a continuing dispute: in Osama bin Laden's view, as evidenced by his invectives against Western or 'infidel' hypocrisy, public opinion in non-Muslim countries offers no effective constraint on violence against the oppressed.

In Fanon's view, the principal resource the oppressed have against oppression is their moral superiority, in particular, their moral virtues resulting in their readiness to sacrifice their own lives for their liberation. In praying for the blessing (or for the elevation to Paradise) of those who sacrificed their lives in terrorist actions against the oppressors, Osama bin Laden appears to be praising the same virtue. According to Fanon, the oppressors, as mentioned above, are constrained by the cost of their oppression. They do not want to pay—nor could they pay more—than the oppression is worth to them. They often consider it not to be worth the loss of too many lives of their own people. If a large number of them or a large number of sufficiently important people are to be killed in the effort to maintain control over the oppressed, they may see the operation as too costly. In short, usually the oppressors are not as ready to sacrifice their lives to maintain oppression as the oppressed are to sacrifice theirs to free themselves from it.[4]

In view of this, the only way for the oppressed to liberate themselves from oppression is to make oppression too costly for the oppressors. Terrorist violence is one of the ways to achieve exactly this. In a situation in which the oppressed group has no organisational framework nor military hardware required to fight the oppressors' armed force, terrorism may be the only way of achieving this. In other situations, in which the oppressed have a fighting force capable of waging guerrilla warfare against the oppressors' armed forces, terrorism may be viewed as the most effective way of increasing the cost of oppression for the oppressors beyond a level acceptable to them. For example, the death of wives and children of the (male) oppressors, caused by terrorist acts and the continued threat of more being killed, may turn out to be too high a price for maintaining oppression. Whether this is the case or not, Fanon regards terrorism as one way—or one aspect—of waging the struggle for the liberation from oppression. The ultimate goal of the oppressed—liberation from oppression— provides grounds for justifying terrorism or the use of violence against those who are not engaged in coercion. What kind of justification is this?

Why terrorism is justified: From the point of view of a liberation ideology

The liberation ideology outlined above appears to offer two quite different patterns of normative justification for terrorism: the first appeals to the alleged right of group retribution, and the second to a means/end justification.

The right of (group) retribution

Since oppression, in the cases cited both by Fanon and Osama bin Laden, involves the use of random or undifferentiated violence against the oppressed, this justifies a response in kind—terrorist violence against the oppressors. This type of justification appeals to the (alleged) right of group revenge or of group retribution: if members of one group indiscriminately kill members of another group, then the latter is justified in indiscriminately killing members of the former in the same way.

The collective definitions of the oppressed/oppressors appear to be specifically designed for the purposes of this type of justification: if all members of a particular group (for example, 'infidels') are considered to be oppressors or supportive of oppression, then this alleged right justifies terrorist killing of any members of the oppressor group, regardless of whether they have actually committed (or were capable of committing) any acts against the oppressed. Thus, in his statements, Osama bin Laden praises terrorist acts as acts of revenge against the infidels who, as a group, subjected the believers (the oppressed) to oppression.

There are two major problems facing a justification of this kind. First, setting up two parallel groups, of the oppressed and the oppressors, does not demonstrate that all members of the oppressor group are equally responsible or are responsible at all for the oppression. Thus, even if one grants that all of the oppressed are equally humiliated by the oppression, it does not follow that all of the oppressors are equally responsible for that humiliation. Some people belonging to this group, such as the infirm and minors, are not capable of being responsible for any of those acts that lead to humiliation or oppression. This justification either requires a concept of responsibility that makes minors or other individuals responsible for acts they cannot even comprehend, let alone commit, or, alternatively, it implies that one is justified in exacting revenge or retribution even against those who are in no way responsible for the oppression. In the latter, alternative case, retribution ceases to be a punishment for a wrongdoing: those who are subject to retribution are no longer those who are responsible for it.

This leads to the second problem concerning the ethical status of this alleged right. While some religious or ethical teachings propound the right of individual retribution—the eye-for-an-eye principle—as a principle of punishment for individuals for certain crimes of violence, it does not follow that a similar principle holds for the punishment of groups. The individual retribution is meted out as punishment to the individual who committed a particular act. But groups or individuals randomly selected from a group are not responsible (at least not in this way) for particular acts committed by specific individuals. Therefore, even if one accepts the principle of individual retribution as an ethical principle, one has no reason to accept an analogous principle of group retribution as a principle of the same kind.

The means/end justification

Terrorism is in some situations the only, and in others the most effective, way to make the cost of oppression unbearable to the oppressors and thus to liberate the oppressed. Since liberation from oppression is the only way of restoring human dignity to the oppressed, this goal justifies the only, or the most effective, way of achieving it.

The end (*telos*)—the restoration of human dignity to some—justifies using the lives of others merely as a means towards that end. In addition to this rather general teleological justification, the above liberation ideology offers four more specific justifications that follow a similar pattern but do not explicitly mention liberation as the ultimate end of terrorism.

1   *Terrorism as a means of attacking the system of oppression.* In spite of posing no threat to the oppressed, family members of the agents of oppression (the actual perpetrators of coercion) are part of the system of oppression and receive its benefits. In attacking family members, the oppressed are attacking the system; and an attack on any part of the system is justified, if it will hasten or contribute to liberation.

2   *Terrorism as a means of equalising the conditions of combat.* The oppressed are not in a position to compete with their oppressors in the field of military technology and organisation; therefore, to require them to target only their military and police is to expect them to accept their combat inequality and to remain oppressed. It is only fair that they be allowed to use those means in which they have an advantage over their enemies: this may involve killing even those who are not engaged in any coercive activity.

3   *Terrorism as a means of mobilising public opinion for the liberation from oppression.* When terrorist acts are committed in public spaces, primarily against civilians, the media of the oppressors' state can hardly ignore them. This may attract attention of domestic and international public opinion. If the public realises how costly and how unjust continued oppression is, this may bring about its early demise.

4   *Terrorism as a means of restoring dignity to the oppressed.* When the oppressed fail to respond to the oppressor's violence and oppression, that failure can be taken to indicate their lack of human dignity. By responding to oppression by unleashing undifferentiated violence (which has also been used against them), the oppressed are throwing off this burden of humiliation and showing themselves to be equal in dignity to their oppressors.[5]

All of the above teleological justifications assume that the ultimate value, at least for the oppressed, is the liberation from oppression and the restoration of their human dignity. Liberation from oppression should enable those who have been prevented from enjoying liberty and dignity to enjoy them as other human beings do. It is because Fanon believed in the value of human liberty and dignity that he urged those who enjoy neither to fight to liberate themselves from the control of their oppressors and from the resulting humiliation. The ethical conception according to which the ultimate value is the restoration of human dignity of the oppressed through liberation may be called *liberation humanism*. Terrorism, in Fanon's view, is presented as a practical means of securing humanist values in the world in which some groups and their members are denied both liberty and dignity.

Teleological justifications of this kind are open to variety of criticisms, some of which are explored by Robert Young[6] and others in this volume. Here I shall only discuss one test of a teleological justification, namely, as to whether the values that define the end (*telos*) are compatible with the proposed means towards that end. The end is here defined in terms of the dignity and liberty that are be restored to the oppressed. But the means, terrorist violence, denies not only the dignity and liberty of the victims of terrorism but also their lives. To avoid the obvious incompatibility between the means and the values through which the end is defined, the liberation humanist is forced to fall back on the oppressed/oppressors distinction. As long as their oppression continues, the oppressors' lives, their liberty and dignity have no equal standing to those of the oppressed. In other words, in virtue of their (alleged) responsibility for the oppression, the oppressors have lost the right to their lives, dignity and liberty that the oppressed have. Since, on this argument, terrorist violence does not deny the dignity and liberty of the oppressors, it is compatible with the values that define the end towards which this violence is a means.

By divesting the oppressors of their rights to life, dignity and liberty, liberation humanism partially (and perhaps temporarily) divests the oppressors of their humanity and thus considers them as ethically unequal to the oppressed. There is, however, no reason to accept an ethical degradation of all the members of the 'oppressor' group and any teleological justifications of violence against them. Why this is so may become clearer if we contrast liberation humanism with humanism of another kind that rejects ethical inequalities among human beings.

Why terrorist violence is not justifiable: Universal humanism

Most of us are familiar with an ethical conception that asserts the intrinsic and equal value of each and every human life. Christianity and other universal religions incorporate an ethical vision of this kind, and its most elaborate secular version is probably to be found in the works of the eighteenth-century German philosopher Immanuel Kant. This conception asserts that:

(a) All human lives are of equal and paramount value.

From this postulate one can further infer[7] that:

(b) The intentional killing of another human being is permitted only in self-defence or in the defence of those who cannot defend themselves.

(c) For the purposes of the above, one can defend oneself or others only against those who are threatening to use physical violence or those who enable them to do so by supplying them with or maintaining their weapons.

In contrast to liberation humanism, the ethical conception based on assertions (a) to (c) postulates the value of human life as a universal value of paramount importance. Hence I will call it *universal humanism.*

Universal humanism endorses or incorporates the ultimate values of liberation humanism: liberty and dignity of the oppressed, to which the latter is committed, is also a high-ranking (although not the highest ranking) value of universal humanism. Those who endorse universal humanism can endorse, without any inconsistency, the goal of liberation humanism—the liberation of the oppressed from oppression. Further, universal humanism can also justify the use of violence (including killing) against those who kill, threaten to kill, or aid the killing of the oppressed: violence of this kind qualifies as self-defence or defence under (c) above. But universal humanism prohibits killing other human beings— regardless of the group they belong to—in pursuit of any other objective except self-defence or defence as defined in (c).

Thus universal humanism rules out only certain means towards the liberation of the oppressed: that of violence against those who are not engaged in any coercive activity. The reason for this is found in its conception of the ultimate value or, in other words, in its ranking of values. For universal humanism the ultimate value is the life of every human being. For liberation humanism, the ultimate value that overrides that of the life of every human being is the liberation of the oppressed. To put it very crudely, liberation humanism holds that the lives of the oppressors are of less value than the achievement of liberation of the oppressed and that, therefore, their lives can be used merely as means or instruments towards that preferred end.

Liberation humanism therefore rejects premise (a)—that each and every human life is of equal and paramount value—that universal humanism shares with a number of religious and secular ethical conceptions. Let us now examine why Fanon and his supporter Jean-Paul Sartre[8] reject universal humanism.

Liberation humanism against universal humanism

Liberation humanism counters the above claims of universal humanism in two complementary ways. First, Fanon and Sartre argue that in practice universal humanism sides with the oppressors by blocking attempts by the oppressed to liberate themselves from oppression and, second, they expand the concept of self-defence to include defence against the system of oppression and thus against anyone involved with that system in any way. The first strategy is foreshadowed in justification (2), which demands that the conditions of combat be equalised. Although universal humanism condemns oppression, it denies to the oppressed the only, or the most effective, means of liberation from oppression that they themselves have. Therefore, universal humanism denies to the oppressed control over the means of their own liberation and demands that, if they cannot liberate themselves in the manner acceptable to universal humanism (which their oppressors actually reject), they abandon their quest for liberation. If the paramount aim of the oppressed is to liberate themselves from oppression by the most effective means they have, it would not be rational of them to deny themselves the only or the most effective means of liberation: from that point of view, the prescriptions of universal humanism appear irrational.

The second strategy, foreshadowed in justification (1) above, consists in widening the conception of self-defence. According to liberation humanism, any system of oppression continuously violates the human dignity of those oppressed and also presents a continued threat of physical violence against them. These violations and the threats of physical violence are equal in gravity to the threats of actual physical violence against their persons. Since it is the system of oppression, and not only particular individuals within the system, that poses these threats, the oppressed are justified in using violence against the system itself. If violence against the system requires—as indicated in justifications (1) to (4)—that those who are not engaged in coercive activities be attacked, then self-defence against this system also justifies terrorist violence.

The advocates of liberation humanism argue, in very broad terms, that universal humanism ignores the very injustice of oppression and the highly unequal distribution of power and resources between the oppressed and the oppressors, and consequently ignores the gravity of the threats to the oppressed. How could universal humanism respond to these arguments?

Perhaps universal humanism need not respond to the accusation that it fails to back up the oppressed and their struggle for liberation. Unlike liberation humanism, universal humanism does not aim to prescribe or justify a particular type of means for achieving any social or political ends, such as that of the liberation from oppression. Therefore, its failure to justify the actions that supposedly lead to the liberation of the oppressed is not a defect of that ethical conception or an objection against it. Admittedly universal humanism does not offer such useful guidance to political action as that offered by a liberation or any other political ideology specifically designed to do just that.

In spite of this, one can still evaluate a particular political action or a type of action by reference to the ethical prescriptions of universal humanism. If a particular type of action—such as terrorist violence—does not accord with its ethical prescriptions, one faces a choice between the prescriptions of universal humanism and that of the liberation ideology which does. In such a case, the choice is not between two rival or incompatible political visions or ideologies, but rather between a political ideology and an ethical conception or vision. If an ethical conception prohibits the use of a certain means towards a preferred political end, it is not required to propose an equally effective replacement for the means it prohibits.

Ethical conceptions, such as universal humanism, can and do constrain political as well as individual actions: they rule out as impermissible certain actions, and rank, in terms of ethical values, other permissible actions. In contrast, liberation humanism appears designed to license a certain type of political action that

other ethical conceptions prohibit. In view of this, one may suspect that liberation humanism is an ethical view specifically
designed to serve a particular political ideology; if so, one could
argue that it offers no judgement or evaluation of political actions
independent of that ideology.

As we have seen above, its adherents retort that universal
humanism is tied to the oppressors' ideology or ideologies as well:
according to them, universal humanism is used to justify non-
resistance to oppression, and in this way serves the needs of
oppressors' political ideologies.

To rebut this charge, it is not sufficient, I think, to point out that
universal humanism, as outlined in (a) to (c), imports no political
criteria or political goals in its evaluative apparatus. It would also
be necessary to show that universal humanism is impartial in its
treatment of political actions that cause the deaths of innocent
people. In other words, it would be necessary to show that universal humanism does not permit actions, carried out by technologically superior states or political groups, which cause the same
kind of harm as is caused by terrorist violence. For example, the
imposition of UN sanctions on Iraq in 1993, which were initiated
and policed by the USA and its allies have probably resulted in the
death of a large number of children in Iraq (to which Osama bin
Laden is referring in his statement). While this is not a case of
intentional killing, had the UN sanctions not been imposed in the
way they were, many Iraqi infants and children would not have
died. In view of postulate (a) of universal humanism, causing
death of innocent people in this way is as unacceptable as is killing
them by terrorist action. While it is possible to refine the evaluative framework of universal humanism to yield an explicit prohibition of actions of this kind, it is not possible to regulate the use
of the tenets of universal humanism in political debate. For
example, its prohibition of intentional killing of innocents has
been used selectively to condemn terrorist violence, while various
types of state-sponsored violence leading to the death of innocents
are, on purpose, exempt from such condemnation. As it offers no
specific practical guidance to political action, universal humanism
offers no recipe for the abolition of hypocrisy or the use of double
standards.

Universal humanism offers only guidance as to which actions
are, and which are not, ethical. However, there are contemporary

political doctrines, such as cosmopolitan liberalism, which also offer practical guidance on political action while following the precepts of universal humanism. This shows that universal humanism does not necessarily obstruct positive political action in pursuit of the liberation of those who are oppressed.

Yet while living in a state that offers effective protection from violence to its citizens, our choice of universal humanism is not dictated by a need to find protection from violence or humiliation but by our ethical commitments. Those who are exposed to violence, and who are seeking ways of protecting themselves, may regard our choice as too risky for them or simply detrimental to their attempts to protect themselves from violence of others. Our choice of this ethical vision does not entitle us, who have relatively little to lose from the choice we make, to tell others who face threats to their lives or liberty that in making their choices they, like us, are obliged to follow the prescriptions of universal humanism. While universal humanism indeed holds for every human being, it is far from clear that it would be in the self-interest of every person to follow its prescriptions in every circumstance.

7

Jihad and Violence: Changing Understandings of Jihad Among Muslims

Abdullah Saeed

In the post-September 11 period there was a concerted effort in certain sections of the Western media to present Islam as a religion of violence and terrorism. In this, the Islamic concept of jihad was particularly targeted and equated with a doctrine of terror against non-Muslims of the world, in particular against the West. In the minds of many, especially non-Muslims, jihad is now closely associated with terrorism. It evokes killing and maiming, bombing, suicide bombing, rage and a crusade against the West. The September 11 attacks on New York and Washington by people assumed to be Muslims provided the basis for the strengthening of the association of Islam and jihad with terrorism, despite the fact that those who participated in the attacks did not represent the views of the majority of Muslims.

Several conflicts of today's world, such as in Kashmir, Chechnya, Afghanistan, Maluku in Indonesia, the southern Philippines and Palestine, are all in some way Muslim-related, and hence associated with the idea of jihad. The United States and the European Union have recently labelled 'terrorist' a number of groups commonly referred to as 'jihad groups', such as Hizbollah in Lebanon, Hamas and Islamic Jihad in Palestine, al-Qaeda of Osama bin Laden, Lashkar Tayyiba in Pakistan, and Laskar Jihad in Indonesia. The FBI's most-wanted list includes mostly Muslim names. To a casual observer, therefore, there is no doubt that the main problem is not the causes for which these groups are fighting but Islam itself, or at least a certain brand of Islam: the Islam of militants and extremists, in particular, the doctrine of jihad in Islam, which allegedly provides the religious justification for the activities of such groups.

This chapter attempts to survey the doctrine of jihad, its genesis in early Islam and development in classical Islamic law, its modern interpretations by key groups of Muslims, and also to highlight the diversity evident in its interpretations. The primary objective of this chapter is to demonstrate that the doctrine of jihad is more complex and differently interpreted by Muslims than is widely perceived. This diversity exists in the treatment of jihad in classical Islamic law and by scholars and thinkers in the modern period; there is no single understanding of jihad. While for some it can be used as a tool of terror, for others it is a doctrine of self-defence and has nothing to do with terror. Given the focus on the issue of jihad in the nineteenth and twentieth centuries, substantial literature by Muslims and non-Muslims now exists on the issue.[1]

Jihad: Its meaning in the Qur'an

The doctrine of jihad has its roots in the Qur'an, which is the Scripture of Muslims, and the primary foundation text of Islam. The Qur'an contains the textual and religious authority for jihad. *Jihad* is an Arabic term from the root *jhd*, which has the root meaning of 'using, or exerting, one's utmost power, efforts, endeavours, or ability, in contending with an object of disapprobation'.[2] Jihad thus means, variously, 'struggle', 'striving for', and 'exertion' or 'expenditure of effort'. The Qur'an uses the term *jihad* several times followed by the phrase *'fi sabil Allah'* (in the way of God).[3] It is a struggle in which the believers (Muslims) are expected to strive with their wealth and 'person' for the sake of God.[4]

This 'struggle' can exist at several levels: to free oneself from sin, bad deeds, thoughts and words, or to purify oneself spiritually (*jihad al-nafs*). A person making such an effort is considered to be engaged in a jihad. Jihad can also mean using one's abilities or skills to support causes considered 'pleasing' in the eyes of God, such as helping one's parents or relatives, or the needy and the disadvantaged, or doing something beneficial for the community. In this, giving of one's wealth for worthy causes is highly valued. This form of jihad is referred to as jihad of wealth (*jihad al-mal*). Another form of jihad is 'jihad of the pen', which means writing to defend one's faith against attacks by religious adversaries. Jihad also means a struggle against oppression and injustice perpetrated against individuals and the community. In this sense, jihad means engaging in activities that may include war. Even in this case, war is only one way to struggle against injustice, oppression and aggression; there are also non-violent means.

On a continuum, therefore, jihad can range from totally non-violent to violent actions. All of these meanings are found in the Qur'an and other authoritative Islamic literature. In different times and circumstances various groups or individuals have emphasised different meanings. For example, the Muslim mystics (sufis) argue that the most important jihad is the struggle against carnal desires and sin; they usually eschew jihad associated with violence. On the other hand, those engaged in national liberation struggles today argue that jihad associated with violence is the most important form of jihad.

Despite the existence of different meanings and understandings of jihad, classical Islamic legal texts often narrowed down the meaning of jihad to 'war'.[5] The classical doctrine of jihad thus became closely associated with the Islamic doctrine of war and peace.

Classical doctrine of jihad

In discussing the doctrine of jihad, classical Islamic law assumes the existence of a unitary Muslim state (known as 'caliphate'), a state that is ruled by Muslims and is considered 'abode of Islam', where Islamic law is supreme. The primary responsibility of this state is defence of its borders, protection of individuals against outside aggression, implementation of Islamic law and norms in the society for its Muslim populace, protection of its non-Muslim citizens from inside or outside aggression, and maintaining essential and basic services as well as law and order. In this, the function of the Muslim state is little different from that of a modern nation-state, with jihad approaching closely the doctrine of self-defence of a modern nation-state.

In Islamic law, jihad as war is permitted mainly for the following: to defend one's homeland against invasion and aggression, for the propagation of religion (not conversion), and to punish those who violate peace treaties. Where there is no threat of invasion, where there is freedom to propagate Islam, and where there is peace between the Muslim state and others, jihad cannot be used. There are differences of opinion in Islamic law as to whether jihad can be waged against non-Muslims merely because of difference in religion. While some argue that this can be justified against 'pagans' and 'idolaters' (but not against those who follow 're-vealed religions', such as Jews and Christians), others strongly assert the opposite. For the latter, the Qur'an prohibits conversion to Islam by force, and therefore it prohibits jihad against non-Muslims simply because they belong to a different religion. It is only permitted in the face of threats or acts of war against the Muslim community.

From the point of the Qur'an, it is persecution and oppression that justify jihad, not difference of religion. In fact, one of the first texts in the Qur'an (c. 622 CE) to permit Muslims to engage in fighting reminded them that this permission was given because they were driven from their homelands and were persecuted:

> Permission [to fight] is given to those against whom war is being wrongfully waged [Muslims]—and, verily, God has indeed the power to succour them: those who have been driven from their homelands against all right for no other reason than their saying, 'Our Sustainer is God'. For if God had not enabled people to defend themselves against one another, [all] monasteries and churches and synagogues and mosques—in [all of] which God's name is abundantly extolled—would surely have been destroyed [ere now].[6]

In another text the Qur'an says:

> Would you, perchance, fail to fight against people who have broken their solemn pledges, and have done all that they could to drive the Apostle [Muhammad] away, and have been first to attack you?[7]

The opponents of the Prophet Muhammad in his native Mecca, in Arabia, drove the nascent community of Muslims out of their homes, expelled them from Mecca, often confiscated their wealth and property, and also oppressed Muslims who remained behind. Permission for Muslims to engage in fighting was thus related to the oppression that Muslims suffered at the hands of their op-ponents at the time of the Prophet (610–32 CE). Once fighting became an instrument at the disposal of the Muslim community in Medina, where the Prophet and his followers fled, Muslims were encouraged to participate in this collective activity in defence of their community and faith against outside aggression.[8]

It is important to stress in this context that the Qur'anic view of fighting is not to take the part of the aggressor. In one verse the Qur'an commands Muslims to fight those who fight Muslims, and immediately after it says 'but do not engage in aggressive behaviour'. In another text the Qur'an instructs that Muslims should not fight against any people with whom they have a peace that is observed:

> [those non-Muslims] with whom you [O believers] have made a covenant and who thereafter have in no wise failed their obligations towards you, and neither have aided anyone against you: observe, then, your covenant with them until the end of the term agreed with them.[9]

However, there are verses in the Qur'an (from about 631 CE, just before the Prophet's death) that appear to command fighting against certain groups of non-Muslims. The tone is harsher because these texts were directly related to the continuous attacks against Muslims and to the violation of treaty terms by those opponents, which thus posed a serious political and religious threat to the Muslim community.[10] The Qur'an commanded the Muslims to face these threats uncompromisingly.

Muslims and non-Muslims have looked at these few verses and argued that, towards the end of the Prophet's mission, the Qur'an was not simply referring to limited defensive fighting, but was instead adopting a more aggressive posture towards non-Muslims, at least certain groups of non-Muslims: 'polytheists' and 'People of the Book' who had no peace treaties with the Prophet *and* were at war with the Muslims.[11] While it is true that the texts related to war and fighting towards the end of the Prophet's mission became harsher in tone, it could be argued that these texts were related to specific political and military circumstances, and the Qur'anic guidelines on the ethics of war still applied.[12] Under no circumstances was jihad, in the sense of fighting, to be used to oppress others and create injustice and what the Qur'an calls *fitnah*, or, one might add, terror. Nor are Muslims to use jihad to advance self-interest or material advantage. The key function of jihad, from the Qur'anic point of view, is removing oppression and injustice from society, as well as defence of the community.

Classical doctrine of jihad as developed in Islamic law

The classical doctrine of jihad developed in the post-prophetic period (the first two centuries of Islam, that is, the seventh and eighth centuries CE). It was developed by Muslim jurists based on the Qur'an, the traditions of the Prophet and the events of early Islamic history in relation to war and peace. When Muslim jurists developed the doctrine, they were functioning in an environment in which Islam was triumphant and powerful—politically, militarily and economically. The Middle East, North Africa, Central Asia, East Africa, and parts of India and Europe were under Muslim political hegemony at the time. People of various religions and faiths in these regions submitted to Muslim political power and were accorded a 'protected' status within the Islamic caliphate. The classical doctrine of jihad assumed the existence of a unified religio-political rule by a single caliph or imam over a unitary Muslim state (caliphate).[13] Many non-Muslims had treaties of non-aggression with Muslim rulers. No other political power could challenge these rulers; all others had to accept this fact.

The Muslim jurists at the time could see only a powerful Islam, which seemed to affect their understanding and interpretation of a number of Qur'anic texts on jihad. Many jurists believed that the earliest texts of the Qur'an (610–22 CE) on non-violence and patience in the face of oppression had been superseded by the later, very few, verses that had a more belligerent tone, even though those same verses belonged to specific temporal circumstances. In discussing jihad they divided the world into three spheres: one of Islam triumphant, one of a peaceful non-Islam, and a third in which aggressive non-Islam remained dominant.[14] This latter, for the jurists, was a legitimate territory of war in which there was the possibility of perpetual military conflict. Thus the classical doctrine envisaged jihad primarily as a doctrine of war between the Muslim state and belligerent non-Muslims, who were not at peace with the Muslim state. The classical jurists understood two different types of jihad: offensive jihad and a defensive jihad.

- Offensive jihad can be waged by the caliph or imam of the unitary Muslim state against the territory of belligerent non-Muslims to extend the borders of the state and to amplify its resources (but not for conversion of non-Muslims to Islam). Without the authority of the caliph or imam, such an offensive jihad is not legitimate.

■ Defensive jihad is used to protect the Muslim community from threats to its wellbeing.[15] Defensive jihad does not require the existence of the caliph or imam. Each individual in the community is under obligation to defend the land or the community when they are attacked.

Given that the condition for offensive jihad was the existence of the caliph or imam of the unitary Muslim state, theoretically the authority for engaging in offensive jihad has not existed for several centuries in Islam, as since the ninth and tenth centuries CE, Muslims have not had the unitary Muslim state as a result of breaking down of the state into many smaller units.

In the classical doctrine there were differences of opinion on whether a jihad could be waged against a party simply on the basis of difference of religion. While some jurists argued that difference of religion was a justification for engaging in a jihad against non-Muslims,[16] other jurists did not consider that mere difference of religion justified a jihad. For them, jihad could be waged primarily for the purpose of defending the territory of Islam, or to repel a potential or actual threat, or where there were obstacles to the propagation of Islam to remove such obstacles or in the case of offensive jihad to extend the borders of the Islamic state. As evidence for this view, they quoted the practice of the Prophet and the early Muslim community, according to which jihad was waged primarily against non-Muslims who were hostile to the Muslim community and posed actual or potential threats to the very existence of the community. Non-Muslims who were on peaceful terms with Muslims, or who were under the protection of the Muslim state, could not be a target for jihad, not least because this was strictly prohibited in the Qur'an.

Related to this was the debate among classical jurists as to whether a jihad could be waged against non-Muslims in order to convert them to Islam.[17] While some jurists argued that certain groups of non-Muslims, such as the polytheists of Arabia at the time of the Prophet, could be 'forced' to convert, others countered strongly that conversion to Islam could not be a reason for a jihad. Conversion was a voluntary act only. This argument was based on numerous Qur'anic texts that prohibited forced conversion to Islam.[18]

For the classical jurists, jihad was a collective duty (*fard kifaya*) on the part of citizens of the Muslim state. From their point of view, jihad was essential to a Muslim state, and there had to be at least some citizens ready to defend the state against those who posed an actual or potential threat. If war became inevitable, an important rule in this doctrine was that, before any combat took place, it was obligatory for the Muslim leader or the general who was in charge of Muslim forces to invite the non-Muslim opponents to convert to Islam. If they accepted, fighting should not occur. If they refused, they were invited to become protected citizens of the Islamic state. If they also objected to this, the third option was fighting.[19]

In the actual conduct of war, non-combatants—women, children, old men, and also priests, hermits, monks and others devoted entirely to religion—should be spared.[20] This was reflected in the first caliph Abu Bakr's (d. 634 CE) instruction to General Yazid b. Abu Sufyan who was sent to conquer Syria:

> I advise you of ten things: Do not kill women or children or an aged, infirm person. Do not cut down fruit-bearing trees. Do not destroy an inhabited place. Do not slaughter sheep or camels except for food. Do not burn bees and do not scatter them. Do not steal from the booty, and do not be cowardly.[21]

In battle, force was to be used only to the extent needed; mutilation of the dead and destruction of property were to be avoided.[22] The ethics of jihad also addressed how to deal with prisoners of war,[23] when combat should take place, and rules of engagement. All of this indicate that jihad, for classical Muslims jurists, was essentially a state issue, largely equivalent to the modern doctrine of defence of the homeland.

Interpretations of jihad in the modern period

The classical doctrine of jihad remained influential up to the modern period. During the colonial period many Muslims under colonial rule felt that jihad was justified against colonial powers, such as the French in Algeria or the British in Sudan and elsewhere. Muslim opponents of colonial powers saw their lands and peoples as occupied and oppressed, and believed that they had a duty to challenge this domination, by force if necessary.[24] The Mahdi of Sudan engaged in a jihad against the British. In Algeria the Algerians fought against the French for over a hundred years until they expelled the French from Algeria. In Indonesia the Dutch were finally expelled following a jihad. Much of this relied on the classical doctrine of jihad.

This classical doctrine, though still influential in the modern debate on jihad, has been reinterpreted by influential Muslim groups in the modern period. Today, unlike the classical period, there is a substantial degree of diversity among Muslims in understanding the notion of jihad. While some Muslims today hold a view of jihad that is purely 'defensive', others have taken up a more militant and 'offensive' understanding of the concept.

Modernist interpretation

The classical doctrine of jihad was strongly criticised by many Western scholars of Islam as well as Christian missionaries in the eighteenth and nineteenth centuries. It was alleged that Islam was a 'barbaric', warmongering and bloodthirsty religion, and that much of its success in the millennium 700–1700 CE had been a result of spreading Islam 'by force'. The Muslim conquests of the seventh and eighth centuries were seen to be to coerce others to accept the Islamic religion, and, indeed, the 'war spirit' was seen to be an essential characteristic of Islam as opposed to Christianity, which was portrayed as the religion of peace and love.

These attacks on Islam required defence on the part of Muslims. Some, whom we will refer to as 'modernists' and who were represented by figures such as Ahmad Khan (d. 1898) of India, attempted to reinterpret the doctrine of jihad in response to these attacks. He and others also of a modernist persuasion such as Moulavi Chiragh Ali[25] believed that Islam did not condone violence and aggression against others. In fact, in their attempt to demonstrate that jihad was merely a defensive tool in the hands of the Muslim state, they substantially limited the scope of jihad. Ahmad Khan rejected the notion of perpetual conflict between Muslims and non-Muslims. He went back instead to the Qur'anic doctrine of jihad as a defensive instrument that can be utilised only if Muslims were banned from fulfilling essential religious obligations like the five daily prayers, fasting and pilgrimage. For him, as long as the colonial power (in the case of India, the British) did not interfere with matters of Islamic faith and religious practice, there was no reason to advocate a jihad against them.[26]

In a sense, Ahmad Khan was serving both Muslim and British interests in India by attempting to build a bridge between Muslims and the British. Especially after the 1857 mutiny, the British distrusted the Muslims as they blamed the Muslims for the uprising. They therefore sought not to give Muslims sensitive government posts, and also avoided recruiting them into the army.[27] Ahmad Khan, however, wanted to maintain the link between the British and the Muslims in order to enable the Muslims to progress *vis-à-vis* the Hindus, who were in the majority and with whom the British felt more comfortable.[28] Ahmad Khan also wanted to present Islam in the Indian sub-continent as a religion of peace, as opposed to the warlike image propagated by the critics. He argued that the Qur'an prohibited conversion by force, and that acceptance of Islam had followed only long after the political conquests, when the conquered peoples came to appreciate how Muslims treated others and to value and understand the faith itself.

Somewhat similar positions were adopted by Muslims elsewhere. In Egypt Muhammad Abduh (d. 1905) also defended Islam against similar criticisms.[29] Like Ahmad Khan, Abduh believed that jihad was for defence only, and that, in obedience to the Qur'an, military campaigns in the name of jihad to convert people to Islam were forbidden, and that such conversions, if occurred, would be invalid. For Abduh, Islamic history itself demonstrated that Muslims did not convert others by force; Islam spread mainly because of its inherent simplicity and rationality. He differed from Ahmad Khan, however, in seeing jihad as justified if Islamic lands were attacked by a foreign power or were threatened by colonial encroachment.

What must be remembered is that Ahmad Khan and Abduh represented a purely defensive notion of jihad, and one that gained ground in the twentieth century. The classical notion of perpetual conflict between Islam and the 'abode of war' (*dar al-harb*) was, generally speaking, not advocated by figures like Khan and Abduh in the modern period.

Maududi–Qutb interpretation

In the twentieth century several thinkers who belonged to the two best-known movements of the period, Jama'at Islami of Pakistan and the Muslim Brotherhood of Egypt, rejected the modernist interpretation of jihad as advocated by Khan and Abduh as being for defence only. Instead, they adopted a broader interpretation than either the classical or the modernist ones. While the classical doctrine of jihad envisioned a war waged by a state against another state, these thinkers believed that jihad implied a doctrine of 'revolution' against tyranny and oppression, as well as a means of establishing an Islamic socio-political order. Abul A'la Maududi explains this as follows:

> In reality Islam is a revolutionary ideology and programme which seeks to alter the social order of the whole world and rebuild it in conformity with its own tenets and ideals. 'Muslim' is the title of that International Revolutionary Party organised by Islam to carry into effect [sic] its revolutionary programme. And 'Jihad' refers to that revolutionary struggle and utmost exertion which the Islamic Party brings into play to achieve this objective.[30]

This social order was represented for Maududi by Shari`ah law or, in other words, the recognition of the sovereignty of God's will in the state. Maududi adopted the broader definition of jihad, which could range from non-violent to violent. Jihad could thus be waged (not necessarily in the form of war) against other Muslims, such as political authorities who were seen to be 'oppressing' Islam by failing to implement a socio-political order based on the Shari`ah.

Thinkers like Maududi severely criticised the modernists' idea of jihad as defeatist and as serving the imperial interests of the West. Maududi in particular took a negative view of the West and of Western civilisation, which he saw as decadent, morally corrupt and antipathetic towards Islam. For him the West posed a major threat to Islam and Muslims, and was the source of their social, political, economic and even intellectual problems. For Maududi it was imperative that Muslims both resist the lure of the West and engage in a revolutionary struggle to assert Islamic values, ideas, laws and social order in Muslim lands. To achieve this, jihad was an essential revolutionary tool.

Maududi therefore took the classical doctrine further, and envisaged a struggle not only against moral laxity in Muslim societies but also against a world that he saw as unjust and corrupt. To some extent he was borrowing on Marxist doctrine as a basis for his understanding of jihad as a revolutionary movement; for example, he refers to Muslims as the 'International Revolutionary

Party'. He rejected ethno-nationalism and argued that Muslims throughout the world constituted an *ummah,* a single world community. Maududi's notion of jihad was therefore tied to the establishment of an Islamic order in the world.

In Egypt Sayyid Qutb (d. 1966) of the Muslim Brotherhood also believed that jihad was a powerful revolutionary instrument. He also attacked narrow ethno-nationalism, arguing, like Maududi, that it was the broader Muslim *ummah* that mattered. For Qutb, nation-states were really artificial creations of the West. Also, like Maududi, he believed in an Islamic socio-political order the objective of which was to establish God's sovereignty on earth.[31] Thus, there is no significant difference between Maududi's and Qutb's concepts of a dynamic, rather than a defensive, jihad. This view of jihad as a revolutionary struggle was further reinforced by the Iranian Islamic revolution of Ayatollah Khomeini.

Militants' interpretation

In the 1970s and 1980s several militant Muslim groups emerged in places such as Egypt and Syria, with some being offshoots of the Muslim Brotherhood. These groups adopted a more militant interpretation of jihad. They adopted some aspects of the classical doctrine, particularly more extreme interpretations, as well as certain aspects of the Maududi–Qutb interpretation of jihad as a revolutionary struggle. The result was a more militant, extremist view. While jihad in the classical doctrine was essentially a doctrine of war between the Muslim state and its adversaries, in the understanding of these militant groups it became a doctrine of war between them and their adversaries, be they Muslims, a Muslim state, non-Muslims or the West. Osama bin Laden, for example, declared that perpetual war existed between Islam and the West, in particular the Americans. Muslims who support the West in this conflict are also lumped together with the West as enemies of Islam and thus a legitimate target of their jihad.

In the 1980s and 1990s certain factors played a significant role in further radicalising several Muslim groups such as the jihad in Afghanistan, the intifada in Palestine, other struggles for independence or self-determination, and several religion-based conflicts. The first was an international engagement. Muslims from all over the world participated in the jihad against the Soviets until their expulsion from Afghanistan. Those who participated returned to their countries with not only practical experience of jihad but also with a belief that, if they could defeat a superpower, they could also defeat the Muslim states which were waging a war against political Islam, for instance, Egypt or Libya. The intifada also radicalised a large number of Palestinian youth, who decided that violence was the only approach that Israel would understand in their struggle for independence. In addition, the feeling of Muslims of being under siege was reinforced by the conflicts in places such as Kashmir, Kosovo, Bosnia, and Chechnya, especially where the Western powers were seen as providing tacit or open support for anti-Muslim actions.

Given the military power of what were viewed by the militant groups as Islam's opponents—that is, the governments of India, Serbia, Russia, Israel, the Philippines—it was believed that all possible means had to be found to defeat the enemy, including terror against non-combatants. Suicide bombing came to be a weapon of the weak in the face of unequal power, despite the Islamic ethics of war and prohibition on suicide. The concept of 'combatants' was redefined to include all who were citizens of a country and paid taxes that enabled the state to engage in 'oppressive' activities against Muslims.

However, this new militant interpretation of jihad, with its legitimisation of terror against non-combatants and suicide bombing, has been objected to by a large number of Muslims—scholars, thinkers and jurists alike. Muslim religious authorities in most Muslim states have rejected as un-Islamic the targeting of non-combatants, even in the case of an independence struggle. The Organisation of Islamic Conference, which represents all Muslim states, categorically rejected this militant interpretation and declared, for instance, the September 11 attacks to be Islamically unacceptable, indeed, prohibited. In contrast to the militant groups, Muslim scholars and leaders are opting for a new interpretation of jihad, which to a large extent ignores several key aspects of the classical doctrine of jihad and rejects the militant's interpretation of jihad.

Emerging new interpretation with a broad appeal

This new interpretation of jihad has emerged against the increasing militancy of a small number of Muslim extremist groups around the world who call for jihad against both Muslims whom they consider to be apostates or 'not sufficiently Muslim' and Muslim states that, according to the militants, do not 'implement Islamic law'. Needless to say, these extremist groups also call for jihad against non-Muslims and Western countries that they consider to be 'oppressing' Muslims and supporting 'anti-Muslim' activities. The key aspects of this new interpretation appear to be as follows.

Jihad is essentially a doctrine of self-defence. It can be used only by a Muslim state against imminent and certain aggression by an enemy. In this, jihad is equivalent to the doctrine of self-defence in a modern nation-state. It can also be declared in a liberation struggle, as was the case in Afghanistan after the Soviet occupation. It cannot be declared against a Muslim or Muslims or a Muslim state, thus denying the legitimacy of militant-extremists' declaration of jihad against other Muslims or Muslim states. A jihad cannot be declared against a person or a community just because they belong to a different religion. Thus Jews, Christians, Buddhists, Hindus and others cannot be the target of a jihad simply because of difference of religion. Neither can a jihad be declared by a group of Muslims against a nation that has peaceful relations with Muslims. Thus calls for jihad against a state like the United States are considered illegitimate, as these states are part of an international order that submits to the Charter of the United Nations and generally speaking promotes peaceful relations with others. This interpretation also rejects the idea of an offensive jihad as not in line with the Qur'anic commands for non-aggression.

In this interpretation, certain tactics used by militants in what they consider to be a jihad have been rejected. Killing innocent civilians (be they Muslim or non-Muslim), suicide bombing, causing destruction, injury and loss of life of innocent civilians, as well as bombing and destroying public buildings and property, are all seen as against the Qur'anic and prophetic guidelines on jihad and therefore un-Islamic. This interpretation envisages a peaceful co-existence between Muslims and non-Muslims in which life and property are sacred. The condemnation of September 11 attacks by Muslims worldwide largely relied on this interpretation of jihad.

This interpretation of jihad, although it has its roots in the Qur'an, actually began to evolve in the nineteenth century. It gradually acquired its current form in response to a new set of geopolitical as well as social and religious circumstances of the nineteenth and twentieth centuries, as well as the emergence of a more liberal-minded Muslims who argued for rethinking a number of classical doctrines in Islamic law, including the doctrine of jihad. Further stimuli have been the emergence of militant Muslim groups, particularly from the 1970s onwards, and, more recently, the September 11 attacks on the United States. It is important, however, to mention that there are Muslims who do not adopt this interpretation. However, such Muslims appear to be relatively small in number against a large majority that does not share the militants' interpretation.

Conclusion

The Qur'an is clear that war is justifiable in defeating oppression and injustice and in protecting one's homeland and faith; that is, war is largely defensive and precautionary, and is governed by a code of ethics. Classical doctrine of jihad by Muslim jurists chose to focus largely on verses that were more aggressive in tone, and built a doctrine based on their reading of the Qur'anic texts in the light of the socio-political context of the time. This classical doctrine was largely abandoned by the modernists, who were influential in the Muslim world in the late nineteenth and early twentieth centuries. They favoured a defensive understanding of jihad. This, however, was challenged by some very influential Muslim groups, who again modified the doctrine in line with their idea of a revolutionary struggle to make God's sovereignty supreme in an otherwise evil world. But events from the 1970s to the 1990s in several parts of the Muslim world, in particular Palestine and Afghanistan, led to the emergence of a militant reinterpretation of jihad in a struggle against imperialism, neo-colonialism and authoritarianism, an interpretation that relies on more extreme and militant interpretations of jihad in both the classical and modern periods. Muslim scholars and thinkers around the world, however, have rejected the militant interpretation in favour of a non-militant one that gathers in some of the classical ideas, and moves towards that defensive doctrine under which jihad can only be used to defend Muslim homelands against direct aggression. The doctrine of jihad as part of the process of human thinking has changed in response to temporal circumstances and is expressed in disparate forms.

8

Terrorism and the Right to Wage War

Janna Thompson

Are terrorists criminals or combatants? Should their acts be compared to the bombing of Dresden or to the misdeeds of Mafia bosses and drug barons? Should they be judged by the ethical standards of just war theory or by the criminal code?

Government officials generally insist on treating terrorist acts as offences against the law of their land and punish offenders as criminals. But those labelled as terrorists prefer to present themselves as combatants in a war and demand that they and their actions be judged accordingly. Some people have believed that the distinction is worth dying for. Members of the IRA held in the Maze prison in Northern Ireland went on hunger strikes in pursuit of the right to be treated as prisoners of war rather than as criminals.

Most definitions of 'terrorism' do not tell us how the issue should be decided. Igor Primoratz says that terrorism is 'the deliberate use of violence, or threat of its use, against innocent people with the aim of intimidating them, or other people, into a course of action they otherwise would not take'.[1] This definition fits the intimidatory tactics of the Mafia as well as some of the actions of the IRA and other political groups. C. A. J. Coady includes in his definition of a terrorist act the idea that it is 'a political act, ordinarily committed by an organized group',[2] but acts done for political reasons can be criminal. Indeed, some of the actions of drug barons or Mafia bosses count as political in so far as their intent is to influence or control government officials.

Making a decision about how terrorist acts should be classified will not settle the debate about whether terrorist acts are always immoral. By classifying terrorist acts as crimes we are not necessarily condemning them. Acts can be technically criminal and yet morally justifiable. Laws can be oppressive or discriminatory, and it is not always wrong to break them. Some terrorist acts could be regarded as violent and extreme forms of civil disobedience or protest, and the moral debate would then centre on whether such responses to injustice can ever be justified. On the other hand, by allowing that terrorist acts can be acts of war we are not necessarily condoning them. Not all actions are permitted in war, and the part of just war theory that tells combatants what is morally permissable rules out murderous attacks on non-combatants.

Why should it matter whether we classify terrorist acts as crimes or acts of war? One reason why it mattered to the IRA prisoners is because being a combatant carries with it a status as well as some privileges. The IRA prisoners had been accorded special privileges as members of a paramilitary organisation. They did not have to wear uniforms or do prison work. The revoking of these privileges led to the hunger strikes. Criminals are tried and punished in accordance with the procedures of the country in which their offence was committed. There is usually no question about the right of the state to do this. Being a prisoner of war does not necessarily prevent a person from facing a criminal trial. Even ordinary soldiers can be accused of war crimes. But by being classified as prisoners of war individuals come under an international convention. Their treatment is subject to international scrutiny, and it is not clear that the government of the country in which they committed their acts has the moral or legal right to try them for war crimes or to extradite them to stand trial. Many people believe that war criminals should be tried by an independent tribunal.

On the other hand, in most countries criminals have rights that prisoners of war do not possess. They cannot be held without being charged, or incarcerated indefinitely without trial; if they are found innocent of crime they must be released. Prisoners of war can be interned so long as hostilities continue, whether they are guilty of war crimes or not, and governments have sometimes tried to justify detaining people without charge or trial on the grounds that they are suspected or potential combatants. The US government justifies the measures it has recently adopted to detain without trial or try in a military court those suspected of being members of the al-Qaeda network as a reasonable response to the war that this organisation is allegedly waging on America.

Whether terrorist acts are classified as criminal or acts of war is also important because it has a bearing on how we morally judge these actions. Just war theory permits attacks on combatants in war, and these include, according to many people's thinking, officials of state. Immunity from attack by revolutionaries, Coady says, is lost by police officers or political officials who count as agents of oppression.[3] So if a combatant kills such an official as an act of war, then either this is not an act of terror at all, or it is an example of a terrorist act capable of meeting the *jus in bello* requirement that civilians not be attacked (depending on what definition of 'terrorism' we accept). However, if a criminal attacks an official of state, we would not just normally condemn his action (unless there is reason to regard it as self-defence). As A. J. Coates points out, killing a policeman or public official is generally regarded as a worse criminal offence than killing an ordinary person.[4] The same difference applies to other acts that have sometimes been classified as terrorist. Coady regards as terrorist an act that involves 'intentional severe damage to the property of noncombatants or the threat of the same'.[5] If such terrorist acts confine themselves to damage to property then it also seems to be something that might be justifiable in the framework of just war theory (as Robert Young points out).[6] If the damage is done to government property—for example, to a military installation—then, judged in the framework of the just war theory, the act either does not count as terrorist at all (according to Coady), or as a terrorist act that might be justifiable. On the other hand, if these acts against property are properly regarded as criminal, then they can be punished as deeds that contravene the law. Combatants in a war have permissions that ordinary citizens do not share.

A. J. Coates claims that these differences in the way we assess acts of combatants and the acts of non-combatants who break the law are signs of a fundamental moral distinction, usually ignored in discussions about terrorism, between those who have a 'right to war' and those who do not. If we think that terrorism is always (or usually) wrong because it violates the rights of innocent persons, then we make 'an enormous, and almost always unwarranted, moral concession, since the distinction between combatants and noncombatants is one that applies only to a state of war'.[7] For a state of war to exist, he insists, combatants must be able to claim legitimate authority to wage war. If they lack this authority, then the permissions of just war theory do not apply to them. Those who commit violent actions and do not have a right to war are presumably simply criminals, and should expect to be treated as such.

Coates does not provide a definition of terrorism, but a characterisation that seems compatible with the emphasis he places on having a right to war is as follows: 'Terrorist acts are acts carried out by an organisation that does not have the right to wage war and which involve violent attacks on people or property which cannot be justified as self defence'. To be entirely adequate this definition would have to be more specific about the kind of attack and perhaps about the purpose of the action. This understanding of terrorism has implications that are contrary to the views of some of those who have entered into discussions about how terrorism should be defined. The first implication is that acts of combatants are never terrorist—though they may be war crimes. The bombing of Dresden, however unjustifiable, was not a terrorist act. The second is that attacks on police, military officials and installations count as terrorist. Since acts of terrorists are not acts of war their attacks on officials cannot be justified in the just war framework as legitimate acts of war. So, if an appeal to self-defence cannot justify violent acts against officials, then these attacks have to be regarded as directed against innocent people. Nevertheless, a definition of terrorism that appeals to legitimate authority is, I think, closer to the common view of what it is. Terrorist acts are not merely violent attacks on innocent people. They are outside the framework of moral conventions that are supposed to govern war and political relations.

What does it take for an organisation to have legitimate authority to wage war? To be a legitimate party to a war, Coates insists, it is not enough that a group be organised, in control of acts done in its name, and possessed of a political aim (criteria that, presumably, could be satisfied by al-Qaeda as well as by the United States). A legitimate authority, he believes, is a good international citizen, one that properly represents its people and acts according to law: 'A state's right to war derives not from its de facto or "coercive" sovereignty . . . but from its membership of an international community to the common good of which the state is ordered and to the law of which it is subject'.[8] This law exists as much in war as it does in peace. In Coates's view, even an act of self-defence has to be seen as upholding the law.

There are several problems with Coates's characterisation of legitimate authority. One is that it presupposes the existence and legitimacy of international law and values these laws are supposed to uphold. But if these laws and values are embodied by those practices and agreements that now order the international world, then it seems that some groups of people (particularly non-state groups) can legitimately claim not only that this international order is unjust but that they are not adequately represented by it: that it is a regime whose nature is determined and governed by the powerful. Why should their right to war depend on accepting the legitimacy of something they regard as unjust? If the law Coates refers to is something ideal—not necessarily what now exists but something more just—then it is likely that states or organisations of other kinds will have different ideas about what that should be.

The second problem is encapsulated in the ambiguous term 'right to war'. Coates claims that states are authoritative in so far as their actions 'can be convincingly construed as a defence of the international order and a securing of the common international good', and he compares the state that has recourse to war with a citizen exercising the right of self-defence or making a citizen's arrest.[9] States have legitimate authority, according to him, only if they are acting in defence of law. But this requirement threatens to collapse the distinction between having a just cause and being a legitimate authority. The implication of this idea is that states and organisations that are deemed to be fighting an unjust war—that is, violating the 'law'—have no legitimate authority, and presumably all their attacks on persons and property, military or non-military, count as criminal, and, according to the above definition, as terrorist. Those who have the law on their side would have to be conceived as conducting a police action against a party that is engaged in unlawful behaviour. By making subservience to the law a necessary condition of having legitimate authority, Coates seems to have turned just war theory into a 'just policing theory' for international society.

Whatever the virtues of such a theory, it is not, I think, in accordance with the purpose of just war theory, as Coates describes it in other places,[10] or compatible with the political environment to which just war theory is supposed to apply. The political world to which the theory is supposed to apply is not a Hobbesian state of nature. Moral restrictions on behaviour are possible. It is not a lawless world. On the other hand, there is no universal agreement on how this law should be interpreted and applied. Agents have different ideas about what should be recognised as law, and no agent has the authority, moral or political, to impose its interpretation on the rest of the world. Moreover, the self-interests of the parties will sometimes tempt them to overstep the limits of law, as this is usually understood, or to make an exception for the sake of what they regard as a greater good.

Just war theory presupposes that agents aspire to, and can achieve, peaceful, law-abiding relations, but recognises that a state of affairs in which each agent is entitled to interpret the law for itself and in which there is sometimes a good reason for disobeying existing conventions, is not conducive to perpetual peace. War will occur, and, since interpretations of justice differ and few states act entirely justly, most belligerents will be able to make a case for saying that their cause is just. Even when they are wrong, it is usually not difficult to understand why they could believe in the justice of their cause. Just war theory insists that wars should be waged with the expectation of making a peace in which former belligerents can establish relations of mutual respect and trust, make the compromises and concessions that are required for the maintenance of such relations, keep the agreements that arise from this settlement, make reparation for any injustices they have done in war, or at least take steps to ensure that these injustices will not recur. Just war theory tells us how belligerents who respect both each other's entitlement to exist and important human values should behave in war so that respectful relations can be maintained and peace eventually negotiated and maintained. It presupposes the willingness of belligerents to accept this end and the moral restrictions that make its achievement possible.

In the context of just war theory, so understood, it is reasonable to insist that a belligerent must satisfy three conditions in order to count as a legitimate authority. First, it must be an organisation in control of the violence of its members; it must be able and willing to enforce obedience to the restrictions of just war theory, to negotiate a peace and to keep it. Second, it must recognise (even if it does not always live up to) the restrictions of just war theory, the rights of other parties, and the framework and institutions that make it possible for agreements to be made and kept, and thus for there to be an enduring (if not 'perpetual') peace. To this extent organisations that count as legitimate authorities have to regard themselves as subject to law, though they may have disagreements about the nature of this law and may not on all occasions be law abiding. And third, in making war or negotiating a peace, leaders have to represent the members of an organisation and those for whom the organisation claims to be fighting. War cannot be waged on the whim of a leader or for the sake of some personal cause.

How these conditions should be interpreted and applied would require considerable discussion. Nevertheless, as stated they provide a basis for distinguishing acts of war from terrorism. According to the first condition, those violent acts that political authorities cannot or do not control are terrorist. They are lawless, not only in the sense that they may violate what most people regard as human rights, but because they will not necessarily be reined in or halted by negotiations of political leaders. The suicide bombings now being committed by Palestinians may come into this category. It seems doubtful that these acts are within the control of Yasser Arafat's government, and Israel will probably not be able to bring them to an end just by negotiating a peace with Arafat (though this does not mean that his government is not a legitimate authority in respect to other matters). Acts that are attributed to a particular organisation but in reality are directed and encouraged by another agency also fail this condition. CIA sponsored and directed acts of political violence in Central and South America are examples.

The second condition, that the belligerent must be willing to respect other parties, take seriously the restrictions of just war theory, and accept the institutions and agreements that enable enduring peace to be negotiated, is apparently weaker than the requirement imposed by Coates. It permits a distinction to be made between just war theory's insistence on legitimate authority and the requirement of having a just cause. Nevertheless, it can be used to label some organisations as terrorist. The al-Qaeda network, with its apocalyptic view of a world struggle between Muslims and the West, does not appear to be an organisation prepared to make a peace that respects other parties.

States can also fail to satisfy this condition. Germany under the Nazis was uncompromising in its struggle for the domination of Europe and the enslavement or destruction of those deemed to be of an inferior race. It was not prepared to accept any peace or abide by any agreement that did not meet its terms or to respect the existence of other nations or peoples. Its lack of legitimate authority was reflected in the way it was treated by the Allies. They did not regard the Nazi government as a body that had a right to negotiate a peace. They not only insisted on removing it, they subjected its leaders to criminal proceedings, they investigated its officials for Nazi sympathies, and, even if not directly guilty of crimes, Nazi officials were supposed to be punished by being removed from their posts and forced to go through a period of de-nazification (though for pragmatic reasons this did not happen). In other words, the Nazi government was (most think, rightly) regarded as a criminal organisation.[11] It follows from my definition that all of the violence of the Nazis, including violence against armed forces of the Allies was terrorist—what the Nuremberg judges deemed to be 'crimes against peace'.

To satisfy the third condition it would be too narrow to insist that an organisation must be democratic, but there must be reason to think that in waging war and making peace it is acting according to the will of the people it purports to represent or defend, and that they have some kind of control over what it does. It is not enough that an organisation claims to be acting in the interest of a people. It is not even enough that its actions are widely applauded by people they claim to represent. The organisation has to be accountable to the people; and the people must be prepared to be accountable for the actions it does. The Baader Meinhof gang that attacked military installations in Germany and the Red Brigade of Italy did not represent the people on whose behalf they claimed to be acting. Even if we think that these organisations had a good cause—that the things they were protesting about were really unjust—it is difficult to deny their states the right to prosecute them as criminals. The al-Qaeda cannot claim to represent Muslims, even though some Muslims agree with its point of view.

The condition of being a proper and proved representative of a people seems to favour established states over resistance fighters, revolutionary organisations, or secessionists. Those who rebel against their state often have to organise in secret; they are in no position to demonstrate that they truly represent the people on whose behalf they are fighting. On the other hand, if the uprising is a mass action, then the deeds committed by the revolutionaries will probably not be under the control of any political authority and will not satisfy the first condition. It is inevitable, I think, that just war theory in its application will have a conservative bias. It favours conditions that enable peace to be made, and will generally fall back on established laws, practices, political frameworks, and agents. However, the distinction between acts of war and terrorism does not favour states because they are states. States can be terrorist organisations. Leaders can commit terrorist acts against their population. On the other hand, some revolutionary organisations have demonstrated that they satisfy the condition when they are given a chance to do so. The fact that Bobby Sands, an IRA leader serving a sentence in the Maze Prison, won a by-election as a Northern Ireland representative in the Westminster Parliament, is an indication that many Northern Irish regarded the Sinn Fein, the political wing of the IRA, as representing them. If an organisation is actively supported by a substantial number of the people it claims to represent, then its claim becomes credible.

Distinguishing terrorist acts from acts of war highlights a morally important distinction between violent acts of organisations whose members are able and willing to respect each other in a framework that makes peace possible and those whose actions are, for one reason or another, lawless. However, this distinction rests on a view of the political environment that can be contested. It assumes that there is an international order that political actors ought to maintain. But it also assumes that international society is not like domestic society: it has laws but their interpretation, even their validity, is open to question, and there is no power or government that has the authority to make, interpret, or enforce this law. These assumptions can be contested in two main ways. They will be rejected by those who think that the international order is profoundly unjust and can only be changed by violent revolution. Those who are committed to defending international conventions and institutions, or to the project of peaceful reform of international society, are justified in opposing those who stop at nothing to bring about their idea of a good international society and have no respect for the existence and values of other parties. But the right of leaders to defend international law and order against those they label as terrorists brings with it the obligation to recognise and do something about the respects in which this society is unjust and fails to properly represent many of the world's people.

The assumptions about the world made by just war theory will also be opposed by those who think that recent changes in international society have made it into a society of laws and institutions for enforcing them—something that resembles domestic societies—and that any acts of organised violence count as a violation of this law and deserve to be punished by those who act on behalf of international institutions. According to this view, contemporary wars are really police actions in which the United Nations or the United States and its allies subdue and punish those guilty of breaking the law. This idea of what international society has become amounts to a rejection of the understandings that inform just war theory. Whether it is right requires much more discussion. However, those who hold this view should at least try to avoid trading on a conceptual confusion. If leaders of the United States regard themselves as engaged in a police action against al-Qaeda and the Taliban, then they should favour trying those suspected of terrorism as criminals according to the laws and requirements of criminal justice. There may be reasons in an emergency to suspend some of the provisions that protect those accused of crimes. What can't be justified is to claim that terrorists and their supporters are criminals, and then to treat suspected terrorists as prisoners of war: to lock them up without recourse to law or to try them in special military courts as suspected perpetrators of an unjust war. This policy illicitly borrows justifications from a discourse that has been explicitly rejected by labelling the acts of the terrorists as crimes. In practice it amount to a highly questionable violation of the rights of individuals. It affords them neither the civil protections that are supposed to be given to those accused of crimes nor the rights of prisoners of war.

9

Responding Justly to International Terrorism[1]

Michael P. O'Keefe

Terrorism is firmly associated with states—the formation of states, attacks on them, and attacks by states on their own populations.

What are the essential attributes of terrorism? There are many definitions but little agreement on the essential characteristics of terrorism.[2] Most definitions, whether developed by academics or by governments, list some attributes in common. In a general definition constructed from these common attributes terrorism has at least four facets, all of which involve premeditated violence, or threat of violence with the aim of extracting concessions or enforcing rule. Terrorism can involve non-state actors acting against states, non-state actors using violence against other non-state actors, states using violence against its own population, or states using violence against another state and its population.[3]

The concern here is a type of terrorism that became common in the latter quarter of the twentieth century—terrorism employed by non-state actors to achieve political ends through the use of violence in the international arena. 'International terrorism' is used to differentiate this type of terrorism from the other varieties listed in the typology above. Recent examples are the 11 September 2001 attacks on the World Trade Centre and the Pentagon, and the ongoing conflict between Palestinians and Israel. This chapter is not concerned with terrorism internal to a state, which aims to supplant the government and assume sovereignty, or terrorism between groups within the state, which is not directed at the state. It is also not interested in terrorism by states against their own populations or other states, which is dealt with elsewhere in this volume.[4]

This is not a morally loaded definition *vis à vis* the injustices (real and otherwise) that prompt terrorism. There is no mention of either the justice of the terrorist's goals or the moral defensibility of the state, its citizens or the property belonging to either.[5] It does not require a judgement to be made about the legitimacy of a particular state that is the target (victim) of international terrorism, or the terrorist group or population that is the target (victim) of injustice in the international arena. Therefore, this definition avoids the confusion created by value-laden discussions of 'terrorists' and 'freedom fighters'.

This definition can allow analysis to concentrate on acts of terror themselves. It is inclusive enough to allow for instrumental arguments mentioned by those who seek to justify the use of terrorism to achieve a just cause, and also by those who argue that unconstrained counterterrorism can be used to defend a just state (from a utilitarian perspective). 'Unconstrained' is the key word here. Just as instrumental arguments can be used to justify challenges to states using morally dubious tactics, so can they be used to justify morally dubious responses by states to terrorism.

The following discussion is not interested principally in whether terrorism of whatever variety can be justified, but rather in how democratic states should respond to international terrorism. The vastly different implications of international terrorism against democratic versus authoritarian states are often overlooked. Democratic states accept limitations on their behaviour that are challenged by international terrorism. Instrumental arguments that justify removing the self-imposed constraints on the behaviour of states to allow unconstrained counterterrorism will be negated below.

International terrorism and terrorist organisations

Understanding the nature of international terrorism involves answering two questions: Who or what is the object of the attack? Who is the attacker?

The object of the attack

Terrorists use the threat of violence to great advantage. The demonstration effect of attacks, and the threat of more to come, aim to have a greater impact than the actual violence involved. International terrorists use violence and the threat of violence to achieve political ends, short of the destruction of a democratic state. That it primarily aims to strike fear in the population of the target state is often used to differentiate international terrorism from war between states. However, it is not the fear caused by a threat that differentiates the two forms of violence but rather who is targeted.

The targets of international terrorism include elected politicians, government employees, institutions and property, and the broader populace and its property. Attacks against these people and this property can occur either in the targeted state or overseas— diplomats, overseas missions, business interests and tourists. Political leaders, combatants and non-combatants acknowledge that in a war the military potential of their state may be degraded, which could involve some of the former two groups losing their lives. In contrast, political leaders, combatants and non-combatants alike will fear terrorists who are routinely indiscriminate in selecting targets and, in fact, may concentrate on threatening non-combatants. This fear is the reason why groups such as the Palestinians believe that suicide bombing is such an effective method of achieving their aims.

The core issue is that terrorists do not respect the principle of discrimination: the immunity of non-combatants from attack.[6] Terrorists target the population of a state (most of whom are non-combatants) rather than a class of people within the state (combatants).[7] Some theorists argue that the distinction between combatants and non-combatants broke down in the twentieth century with the advent of total war.[8] This debate is only tangential to the argument here, and the focus will remain on a distinction between legitimate and illegitimate targets. Legitimate targets are military personnel and those civilians who are directly involved in preparations for war.[9]

It is almost unavoidable that some non-combatants will be casualties, but the point is that non-combatants should not be made the targets of international violence. Efforts must be made to ensure that they are not placed in harm's way. International terrorist organisations do not accept these types of side constraints on their behaviour. It is ironic that, while states have been focusing more on using technology to limit 'collateral damage' in war, the use of indiscriminate violence by international terrorists has been growing in intensity.

The moral significance of non-combatants or 'innocents',[10] and the common repulsion over their deaths in war, has led to their status being enshrined in national and international laws. The immunity of non-combatants from military attack is the cornerstone of just war theory, as it relates to the conduct of war (*jus in bello*). By contrast, terrorists do not acknowledge these moral limits on their actions.[11] They do not accept the conventions that represent a form of international morality that has developed over the centuries in the Westphalian state system.[12]

Only under very specific and limited situations is taking another person's life justified. The one thing that these situations have in common is that the killing is not indiscriminate. There is a 'categorical prohibition of murder' in national and international laws. This prohibition is shared by various moral frameworks and perspectives.[13] It is not constrained by national boundaries.

The use of violence against non-combatants across borders is illegal under national and international laws. In either jurisdiction self-defence and the defence of the defenceless are the clear justifications for taking another life, and in the case of international terrorism the violence involved fails this test. Some may seek to excuse terrorists who exclusively target property or selectively assassinate political leaders;[14] however, the empirical evidence of terrorist acts does not support this distinction. Most acts of terror either recognise the moral necessity of avoiding casualties amongst non-combatants but find justifications for weakening this prohibition, or directly aim to harm or kill non-combatants.

We will see below that a lack of discrimination between combatants and non-combatants by non-state actors tempts states to operate outside the framework of just war when responding to this form of violence.

Who is the attacker?

Seldom is international terrorism attributed to an individual acting alone. An individual may lead or bankroll a terrorist act or campaign but an organisation is needed to successfully achieve it.

Terrorist organisations do not have the status of states in the international system but they do posses some attributes of states. They possess institutional structures that allow them to manage operations involving large numbers of resources, both capital and human. International terrorism is becoming a more complex undertaking requiring, among other things, long-term planning, high-quality intelligence, committed personnel and large amounts of funds.

Many terrorist organisations are sponsored by states. In the latter half of the Cold War the United States levelled this charge at the Soviet Union, but at the end of the Cold War the emphasis shifted to Islamic states. However, this does not mean that all international terrorist groups simply act as a state's irregular military force. If the organisational structure and personnel of an international terrorist group could not be differentiated from those of the host state, then the host state could not 'plausibly deny' involvement in the attack, which could be treated as an act of war between states rather than international terrorism. This type of state-sponsored terror would provoke reprisals, such as in the case of the US attack on Libya in 1986 in response to bombings targeted at US military personnel in Europe. In contrast, most terrorist groups are organisations that can operate independently or alongside state structures. The host state may be unwilling or unable to exercise sovereignty over its entire territory, and the terrorist organisation can gain de facto sovereignty over an area within a state.

Another attribute that states and terrorist organisations share is using, or threatening to use, large-scale violence across international boundaries with the aim of extracting political concessions from a state. To paraphrase Carl von Clausewitz's famous dictum, terrorists use 'war' to achieve political aims.[15] International terrorism is being used by these non-state actors as a new mode of warfare. This attribute clearly differentiates international terrorists from those who operate within a domestic jurisdiction and only aim to influence domestic politics.

It could be suggested that international terrorism is simply guerrilla warfare in an enemy's concrete jungle. However, international terrorism is not a synonym for guerrilla war, although there is some crossover between the two. One reason for confusion is that some incidents labelled terrorism actually represent guerrilla warfare, such as in the case of the 1983 bombing of US forces in Beirut. The central difference between the two is that guerrilla warfare routinely involves asymmetrical attacks by irregular forces against an occupying military force in an occupied territory rather than attacks against the metropolitan territory or population of the occupier. Guerrilla attacks also occur from groups claiming sovereignty in the occupied territory (or denying the legitimacy of the occupier) rather than organisations aiming to achieve non-territorial diplomatic goals, such as influencing how the target state conducts its foreign relations. An attack by the Shining Path against Peruvian military forces within Peru is more likely to be viewed as guerrilla warfare and a bombing of a restaurant in Tel Aviv by a Palestinian group is more likely to be judged as terrorism.

International terrorism is analogous to what is termed low-intensity conflict or state terrorism between states. States have prepared for this type of irregular warfare for many years.[16] That is, military methods are used to achieve diplomatic results (which do not necessarily involve territorial gain against the target). The methods are similar to guerrilla warfare, but do not limit their tactics to the defeat of the target's military forces in occupied territory. It may be that the instrumental justification for terrorism is more suited to justifying guerrilla war than acts of international terrorism.

International terrorism does not simply involve an isolated attack. It involves an orchestrated campaign of violence where the casualties and destruction of property are similar to the outcomes of contemporary low-intensity conflict. However, unlike low-intensity conflict, military personnel are not the primary targets of these attacks. For good examples of the trend toward the large loss of life and destruction of property we need only review the attacks in the last ten years on residential areas in Moscow or on the US embassies in Africa and the World Trade Centre. Furthermore, the use of weapons of mass destruction by international terrorists could cause vast numbers of non-combatant casualties.

Terrorist organisations may not possess these attributes to the same degree, but they are identified by them by the states that they threaten. Terrorists also view themselves as possessing some of these attributes. In practice the threat and use of violence by terrorist organisations leads them to be treated as quasi-states by democratic states. Conflating a non-state actor with a state is contentious, but it accurately reflects the way these non-state actors assume some of the attributes of states that relate to the use of violence in the international arena, and reflects the fact that states treat these actors as quasi-states. Regardless of the definitional ambiguities relating to the description of the aggressor, states are responsible for defending their citizens from external threats. The corollary of this argument is that terrorist organisations may feel responsible for protecting the interests of their followers, and this should be factored into responses to terrorism.[17]

Terrorists as international law-breakers

The use of international terrorism as a mode of warfare raises a number of difficult questions for decision-makers, not the least of which is how to respond to threats from non-state actors whose use of force is considered illegitimate. The issue becomes more complex because these terrorists are resident in another state and acting against them without the 'host's' consent would be prohibited. States aim to limit the ability of terrorists to achieve their political ends through the use of morally dubious strategies, but how can they bring international law-breakers to justice?

Historically they have concentrated on punishing law-breaking in their domestic jurisdictions and law breaking that occurs in relations between states. In contrast, less effort was dedicated to resolving how to respond to military threats from non-state actors. There has been great debate over whether national or international laws should be used to bring terrorists to justice.[18] In the case of contravening national laws, the use or threat of violence against the state or its citizens by a resident of that state is treated as a common crime (murder, extortion, treason, and the like), and these offences have evidentiary requirements and punishments based on national laws (such as in the case of the Oklahoma bombing in 1995). In the case of breaking the laws of war, clear conventions have been developed to regulate the behaviour of states and create a sense of international community from as early as the Treaty of Westphalia in 1648.

The treatment of threats from non-state actors across international boundaries is not so clear. The targets of international terrorism are located within a state or are under a state's jurisdiction because a state possesses the legitimate monopoly of force in a delineated area (this includes 'flagged' ships, aircraft from the national airline flying overseas, and diplomatic missions). The state is responsible for responding to the use or threat of force in its jurisdiction. If someone is harmed within the state by someone within that state's jurisdiction they will be tried under local laws in local courts. States are also responsible for trying terrorists resident in their jurisdiction who attack the citizens or property of another state. However, if terrorists reside in another state that is not willing or able to exercise jurisdiction, or if they are stateless persons, then their status is unclear.

International terrorism is unlawful in so far as it (a) breaks the laws of the target state, *and*, as discussed earlier, (b) the terrorist organisation is treated as having some attributes akin to a state, which means that the terrorist organisation is responsible for breaking the laws of states (or can be treated as not obeying any laws). As such, international terrorism is a challenge both to the legitimacy and authority of national political communities and to the international system, which relies on the reciprocal respect of the sovereignty of states.

The definition of international terrorism developed earlier was designed to avoid making moral judgements about the reasons terrorists use to justify their actions, but does identify terrorist violence as being criminal. It is not the reasons for using violent means but the type of violent means used by terrorists that differentiates terrorism from the lawful use of force. International terrorist organisations are law-breakers because they illegally use military force to target non-combatants in the international arena.

Terrorist attacks are judged by the victim to be profoundly unjust and illegal, not necessarily because of the reason for the attack, but because it does not conform to the 'civilised' rules of warfare. It involves the illegal and illegitimate use of violence against non-combatants in the international arena. (This argument is often made in discussions of September 11: some groups in the Middle East may have had legitimate grievances but the methods they used were inappropriate and unlawful). Despite general agreement on the illegality of international terrorism there is debate over the procedures that should be applied to trying terrorists, with the implication that military tribunals and the like would relax evidentiary standards developed in domestic law.

It is not clear who has jurisdiction over international crimes. A large number of international laws and conventions dealing with international terrorism exist, but either they either do not contain strict enforcement mechanisms or they are seldom enforced.[19] Often states do not 'either extradite or punish' those accused of political crimes by another state.[20] Ideally the United Nations (UN) should act as the arbiter of international disputes (as it was intended) but ideological and other divisions have rendered it an imperfect device for co-ordinating collective action to protect states, especially from international terrorism.[21] Similarly, attempts to establish an International Criminal Court with universal jurisdiction have been stymied by the resistance of states such as China, the United States, and Russia. If the UN or an effective international court are excluded for practical reasons, this leaves states to develop their own responses to international terrorism. This does not mean that we should give up on multilateral approaches to terrorism, but they must be treated as an 'ideal' method of combating terrorism. As it stands, multilateral approaches legitimise bringing international terrorists to justice but the means of doing so have generally been unilateral.

The question is, what principles should apply to military responses by states to illegitimate terrorist attacks?[22] If we conflate international terrorist organisations with states, then this question has been posed before: What principles should guide states in fighting a just war against an enemy using unjust tactics?

State responses to international terrorism

It is one thing to argue that terrorism is illegal under national and international laws, but the more pointed question is what principles states should use to deal with law-breakers, especially when they are non-state actors that possess some but not all of the attributes of states?

In this section I will begin by reviewing the instrumental arguments for removing the self-imposed limits on the counterterrorist activities of states. (There is also a moral argument that, because of their representative nature, democratic states have a responsibility to respond to the illegitimate use of force against non-combatants in their jurisdiction, but, while this premise should be noted, it is beyond the scope of this chapter.) I will then use the earlier overview of the nature of international terrorism to discuss the appropriate framework within which state responses to terrorism should be framed.

The instrumental argument for unconstrained counterterrorism

Justifications for terrorism often employ an instrumental argument: it is impossible for the terrorists to achieve their *just* aims without resorting to tactics that would otherwise be treated as morally dubious.[23] The assumption is that terrorism is a weapon of the weak used by the oppressed against the oppressors, or by non-Western states against Western states.[24] This may sometimes be the case, and other chapters in this volume deal directly with cases where putting aside principles analogous to just war theory when deciding to mount a terrorist campaign (legitimate authority, last resort, real chance of success, proportionality, etc.) may be justified.[25] However, this justification is misused when it is applied to cases where terrorism is used systematically simply because it is believed to have greater utility than other means of achieving political ends.

The corollary of the instrumental justification for international terrorism is an instrumental justification for unrestrained counterterrorism. Proponents of this position would argue that democratic states are extremely weak and ill prepared to counter asymmetrical threats posed by international terrorism, especially when it involves martyrdom. International terrorists are difficult to target because they are indistinguishable from civilians, and, almost by definition, they fight 'evasive' wars, and lack a geographic area over which they possess sovereignty in which they can be attacked.[26] Terrorists are chameleons who can blend equally well into the population of the host or target state. Furthermore, contemporary democratic states afford their populations and often the populations of other states certain rights by affirming national and international laws. These rights can be abused and manipulated by international terrorists. In this manner terrorists 'challenge the democratic capacity to govern' and to participate in the international community.[27]

An instrumental argument is often used to justify suspending certain moral and legal rights and obligations in the name of national interests—in order to allow democratic states to respond effectively to terrorism.[28] That is, it is argued that military necessity demands that states loosen the limitations on their behaviour when responding to an enemy who does not respect them.

Furthermore, if international terrorists do not acknowledge the foundational distinction in just war theory—the obligation to discriminate between combatants and non-combatants—then states should not have to apply any just war or other criteria to the conduct of counterterrorist operations against them. This line of argument is often used in discussions of just war theory between states and in the case of civil wars. For instance, James Johnson notes that until relatively recently the belief was that 'just war limits do not apply in war against rebels'.[29] It was also widely aired after the September 11 attacks.

The instrumental argument was evident in the Uniting and Strengthening America by Providing Appropriate Tools Required to Intercept and Obstruct Terrorism (USA-PATRIOT) Act passed by the US Congress in October 2001. This Act aimed 'to untie their hands and take the shackles off' the CIA's counterterrorist operations to allegedly make them more effective.[30] This legislation was in tension with the US Bill of Rights and a number of international agreements, and was strongly criticised by European governments.[31] Despite these criticisms most Western states introduced legislation during this period that weakened the limitations on the use of the state's security apparatus to combat terrorism.

Some politicians and academics may argue that it is extremely difficult to defeat terrorism, but does this difficulty justify states using any or all the means that are at their disposal? Frustration over mounting an effective response to terrorists often leads to calls to ignore the restraints on behaviour that are codified in domestic and international laws. This argument suggests that any person or group not operating according to, let alone accepting the legitimacy of, international norms and conventions cannot claim protection from these norms. That is, that no limits should be placed on the operation of the organs of state security in removing this threat to national and international security. For instance, some commentators argue that participating in an act of terrorism questions, and in some cases forfeits, an individual's right to have rights.[32] This line of argument shows the limitations of focusing on the rights and obligations of terrorists. Terrorists operate in an unfamiliar legal and moral space for states, and governments may be tempted to locate terrorists in a moral and legal vacuum, but responding to their acts by simply removing their rights is unjustified. Surely some rights are inalienable. When states respond to international terrorism, it does not matter whether terrorists do not acknowledge the rules altogether or whether they do recognise them but feel justified in ignoring them; what matters is that states have developed norms that guide their behaviour, regardless of the actions of other states or non-state actors.

There is one case, albeit a contentious one, where a state fighting a just war could possibly suspend the laws of war. In *Just and Unjust Wars* Michael Walzer discusses the 'supreme emergency' where the very existence of the state is threatened and it has no recourse other than to employ morally dubious tactics to defeat the threat.[33] There is some debate over the nature of the 'supreme emergency.' A narrow interpretation sanctions the use of these tactics only in the case of a moral disaster, while a broad interpretation recognises the value of defending a unique political community from destruction. At first glance international terrorism does not appear to be capable of representing a case of the former interpretation of a 'supreme emergency', so just war theory would seem to prohibit any relaxation in the laws of war. However, international terrorism could represent a threat to the existence of a state if weapons of mass destruction were used (it could be argued that the destruction of the US government in a surprise nuclear attack on Washington, DC, would represent a 'supreme emergency'.)

While the broad interpretation of 'supreme emergency' appears to give credence to the instrumental argument for unrestrained counterterrorism, it stretches Walzer's qualification to breaking point, and ignores just how contentious the qualification is. The 'supreme emergency' has to be substantiated, and this would be extremely difficult if not impossible in the case suggested earlier. As surprise would be necessary for the terrorist attack to be successful, then it follows that the attack would occur before evidence could be marshalled to argue that the laws of war and other conventions should be suspended. The burden of proof would require that not only are there the capabilities to mount a terrorist attack of this magnitude, but that the terrorists themselves have the intention to launch such as attack. The latter would be much harder to establish than the former. In addition, it would have to be demonstrated that removing the self-imposed limitations on the conduct of states would actually be an effective means of countering international terrorism, which is not as clear cut as it may appear. By contrast, in an orthodox war there could be situations where a state was able to gather evidence of an impending attack that *may*, and I stress *may*, justify taking such drastic action.

National and/or international laws of war apply to state responses to international terrorism. There is a form of international morality that proscribes terrorism. This moral order can be challenged on a number of grounds. It may not represent the groups that practise terrorism, but attempting to modify it to acknowledge the validity of international terrorism as a mode of warfare would be inappropriate and dangerous. States do not have unfettered freedom to respond to (and to pre-empt) terrorist attacks. The populist compulsion to respond to terrorists in kind challenges the ability of moral frameworks embedded in national and international laws to provide answers to the dilemmas raised by international terrorism, and is rejected.

Just war theory and responses to international terrorist organisations

In order to survive and function effectively in the international system, states, in principle, must respect the reciprocal nature of sovereignty, uphold international law, and rely on diplomacy to settle disputes.[34] The difficulty is that this highly militarised spatial conception of security is not designed to cater for military threats that do not come from states and do not necessarily aim to challenge sovereignty over existing territorial entities or create a new state. While states may treat terrorist organisations as quasi-states, states do not go so far as to confer on them the legitimate authority to declare war.[35] There is no declaration of war from a state that possesses the legitimate authority to do so, but rather the unauthorised use of violence in the international arena. For instance, Osama bin Laden did declare war on the United States; however, before September 11 this declaration was not treated with the gravity of a declaration of war from another state.[36]

As states do not confer the legitimate authority on international terrorist organisations, it is not self-evident that rules of war between states apply to state responses to international terrorism. International terrorism appears to be a hard case because it involves similar aims, and the use of the same type of military force, as warfare between states. Traditionally, military threats to states arose from other states, but due to the similarity between terrorist organisations and militarily aggressive states they can be treated using the same legal and moral framework. It is generally acknowledged that legitimate responses to attacks from states should be guided by just war theory, even if these attacks do not adhere to the rules of warfare. The US response to the Japanese surprise attack on Pearl Harbor in 1941 is a good example of this reaction because the lack of a declaration of war did not impact on the conduct of war. It is a measure of the universal applicability of just war theory that these principles can be maintained in the face of attacks from actors who do not respect them.

From the perspective of the targets of international terrorism, terrorist organisations are quasi-states that do declare war on states, but as discussed earlier, the tactics they employ represent a new mode of warfare. Notwithstanding a number of important differences between guerrillas and terrorists, the precedent set by Francis Lieber, *vis à vis* the treatment of guerrilla forces according to just war criteria and international conventions, should be applied to international terrorists.[37] Even though terrorists use the guerrilla tactic of not forming identifiable military forces raised by states, security forces must follow the accepted ways of treating combatants participating in a war. The moral equality that we afford to soldiers, and more recently guerrillas, should be applied to terrorists. Those that are captured or injured should be treated as prisoners of war.[38]

The principle of discrimination should direct military action against terrorist organisations and not those who indirectly support them by harbouring them, for instance. Even if there is a close connection between a terrorist organisation and a pariah state, one that relates uneasily to many states because it does not fully embrace international obligations, it is the terrorist organisation and not the state where it may be operating that should be the target of a just response. This principle can be applied to all states, including some that are currently fighting the 'war against terror' but may have turned a blind eye in the past to the operation of international terrorists within their territory.

Conclusion

The rise of international terrorism displays the limitations of international law and morality in dealing with aggressive non-state actors and raises a number of difficult questions for policy makers.

States have a right of self-defence against international terrorism. In the face of a military threat it is natural for states to attempt to degrade the ability of the 'enemy' to undertake offensive action again. Nevertheless, the difficulty in countering international terrorism should not be used to justify removing or relaxing the constraints on states imposed by just war theory.

The leaders of terrorist organisations should be brought to justice for their role in planning and undertaking terrorist attacks. As terrorist organisations can be conflated with states in regard to the use of violence in the international arena, then terrorists can be treated as soldiers. Just as military personnel involved in crimes against humanity or breaches of the laws of war should be tried for their crimes, so should terrorists. Depending on the gravity of the crimes, they could be tried by international or national tribunals. Capital crimes should be tried by ad hoc international tribunals or the International Criminal Court (using principles established in tribunals that tried war crimes in World War II and in the former Yugoslavia and Rwanda). For lesser crimes, national military tribunals (using the same procedures as are used to try the military under its jurisdiction) may be adequate. The use of military tribunals originally developed to deal with the crimes of national military forces involves an extraterritorial application of domestic laws that is far from ideal, but is not unprecedented. For instance, national laws have been applied to local populations during UN peace operations, notably Australia's jurisdiction over an area in Somalia in 1993.

Aside from the effect on relations between states, it is important that responses to international terrorism do not produce counterproductive reactions in the long term from groups that believe they have legitimate grievances. As Paul Wilkinson has noted in his analysis of terrorism at the end of the Cold War, 'The true Grotian response by Western states to terrorism must combine firmness with a commitment to act within the framework of the rule of law'.[39] More recently, Richard Falk echoed the concern that state responses to terrorism reflect the balance between effectiveness and legitimacy, and do not shift too much toward the former.[40]

States have an interest in encouraging terrorist organisations to accept some limitations on their actions, and terrorist organisations have an interest in ensuring that states do not relax their adherence to the principles of just war. Terrorists may assume that states will not give up their cherished principles, but this belief may be shattered if the terrorist threat increases in degree, as we saw in the legislative responses by states to the September 11 attacks. Nevertheless, the resort to unconstrained counterterrorism would be a disproportionate response. The laws of war must be applied by states to responses to threats from international terrorists.

10

A 'War of Good Against Evil'

Raimond Gaita

Within hours of the attack on the World Trade Centre President George W. Bush and other Western leaders, most notably Tony Blair, said it was more than an attack on the United States, more even than an attack that might justifiably make other nations fearful of their vulnerability to similar outrage. It was, they said, an attack on civilisation. Later, the Americans called their anticipated response 'Operation Infinite Justice'. President Bush has said repeatedly that the 'war against terror' is a 'war of Good against Evil'. Most recently he has identified an 'axis of Evil'.

From the beginning the rhetoric of the Alliance was bizarre, and it continues to be so, almost as apocalyptic as the rhetoric of its enemies. It is a fine thing for a state to seek justice, but even the president of the world's only superpower, in possession of fire-power unprecedented in all of human history, should perhaps leave infinite justice to his God. True, even from President Bush, it is only rhetoric. We have reason to hope that when the crunch comes his policies will be informed by a sharp sense of the difference between the limited, rational goals of an essentially secular state like the United States and the apocalyptic zeal of a state like Afghanistan as it was under Taliban rule. Before the crunch, however, much, perhaps irreparable, damage can be done and many lives sacrificed.

The attack on the towers was an evil deed. Whether the hijackers and all those who supported them are evil, I do not know. But it is certain that none of the nations of the coalition is good, not because any of them is evil, but because goodness of the kind that contrasts with evil and which invites a capital 'G' (the invitation can be declined, of course) is not an attribute of collectives. Goodness of that kind is possessed by saints, whose compassionate love gives the gift of humanity to those whose terrible affliction or terrible evil has made their humanity only partially visible. Collectives, of course, may exhibit fine moral qualities and act with great decency, expressing the compassion of their members, but their deeds never exhibit goodness of the kind shown by saints, and they are never themselves good in the way that individual human beings can be. Collectives, however, can do evil and be evil as Nazi Germany was.

A British journalist (whose name I have forgotten) said that, strange, and perhaps offensive, though it may at first seem, the suicide bombers in the Middle East acknowledge limits to what they may do. The terrorists, he said, who cynically flew the hijacked planes with their passengers into the towers, respected no limits. I suspect he is right. Although at least one of the hijackers professed religious belief, it seems that only someone who is prepared to do anything could do what they did. Their terrible deeds pulverised into dust or burnt into cinders thousands of people, denying their loved ones even the consolation of a funeral. In the dust of the awesome collapse of the towers, which held our attention captive in troubled fascination, many people saw the spectre of a nihilism that would stalk the earth. Perhaps that is why the rhetoric of our political leaders was unrestrained by reality.

In the coming years we will try to understand more clearly what to make of the thought that the attack on the towers (though not, I think, on the Pentagon) marked something new in our political experience. People said in a tone saturated with dread that the world would not be the same again. In an effort to understand the event we will try to place it; we will compare it with others; we will abstract elements from it to see what is essential to it and what is not. It is certain that we will never pare it down to the destruction of highly symbolic, landmark buildings and the murder of almost 3000 people. Always, I am sure, it will be essential to our sense of the event that the building was destroyed by an airliner piloted by terrorists certain that they would die, taking with them the plane's innocent passengers.

The horror of it made a forceful military response imperative for any US president. Bush declared that the United States and her allies will bring Osama bin Laden to justice or bring justice to Osama bin Laden. The disjunction expressed an eloquent confusion. The first part meant, I assume, that Osama bin Laden and his accomplices would be brought to trial; the second that they would be killed. Nine months later, it is unclear whether Osama bin Laden is dead or alive. His assassination would cause few tears in the West, even among those who are sceptical of the part he is alleged to have played in the events of September 11. But it is terrible to hunt him as though he were vermin. That should not be done to any human being, no matter how evil their deeds or how foul their characters.

Increasingly, the belief that members of al-Qaeda are filth and deserve to be treated like filth has betrayed itself in the language of parts of the US military administration, especially in comments by Secretary of Defence Donald Rumsfeld and also by soldiers on the ground. Sadly, it seems that most Americans don't mind that, nor does it matter to them whether Osama bin Laden and his fighters are brought to justice or killed in acts of revenge. It should matter to them, even though revenge is not of itself a bad thing. We tend to think it must be base because we think it is always the expression of a primitive urge to strike back when wounded, an urge that sometimes degenerates into bloodlust. It need not be. In Aeschylus's great tragedy of revenge, Electra, who is driven to avenge her father murdered by her mother, says, 'If the dead are nothing but the dust in which they lay/And blood not paid for blood, then there is no faith, no piety in any man'.[1]

Because revenge can be for the sake of those who are wronged, it can appear to be a requirement of morality, or even as Electra claims, of piety, and it is therefore easily confused with the demands of justice. The trouble with revenge is not that it must be base: it is that there is no natural end to it. Each act provokes a further act, with exhaustion or some other disablement the only limit. As the ancient Greeks were among the first to discover, against the endless cycle of violence motivated by the duty to avenge a wrong, only the institutions of justice introduce a limit of an altogether different kind.

Avishai Margalit, an Israeli philosopher and co-founder of Peace Now, wrote in the *New York Review of Books* that the conflict between Israelis and Palestinians had degenerated into a blood feud.[2] Each side gives forward-looking political reasons for their part in the violence, but in reality each act of violence is motivated by the intrinsically backward-looking nature of revenge.

Disdainful of the administration's embarrassed retreat from a Crusade for Infinite Justice (Muslims were outraged), some hawks in the US military declared they would mount a Campaign of Infinite War. In its way, that gung-ho repudiation of limits—an intoxication that war, or even the serious thought of it, produces in some people—betrayed a nihilism similar to that of the terrorists. For the sake of the civilisation for which the Coalition says it is fighting, it is desperately important that 'the fight against terror' does not degenerate into a blood feud fought in the international arena.

The hawks are winning. Much of the US military and the administration are delighted with the relative ease with which the Taliban and al-Qaeda were defeated. Massive bombing from high altitudes by planes almost invulnerable to attack ensured minimal US causalities. Keen to try the same thing elsewhere, the hawks seem not to understand (or perhaps they are indifferent to) the contempt the United States shows towards its enemies when it kills them in their thousands while denying them the human satisfaction of being able to fight back. They also seem to be blind to the contempt they provoke in their enemies who understandably believe Americans are cowards, only too ready to kill, but not to die. Only a people lacking pride and dignity would allow themselves to be treated as the United States now treats its enemies. The fighters of al-Qaeda may have evil hatred in their hearts, but they are proud. Unable to kill US soldiers, they will hit their enemy in the only place they can—at home.

Many Israelis elected Ariel Sharon to be Prime Minister because they believed that 'force is the only lesson the Palestinians understand'. That escalated a blood feud whose bitter legacy has left both sides afraid to compromise because they think that compromise would show weakness. A high-ranking US official was asked by a British journalist why the United States would not send peacekeeping troops to Afghanistan and why she seemed so little concerned to alleviate the conditions, globally, that encourage terrorism. The American replied, 'You do the peace. We'll do the war'. That attitude may take the world to the same place, bereft of hope, where Israelis and Palestinians now stand.

Writing in the *Guardian*, the Israeli novelist David Grossman described the effect of terrorists on communal life in Israel:

> Just a few weeks of life in the shadow of terror will show every nation that believes itself enlightened just how rapidly and sharply it can turn needs into values, let fear determine its norms. Terror humiliates. It rapidly returns a human being into a pre-cultural, violent and chaotic existence. It determines where society's breaking point is. It entices

certain groups, not small ones, to join it, and to actively seek to use force to destroy and crush everything they hate. Terror contains something that acts like a decomposition enzyme—the decomposition of the private human body and the public body ... A country that fights terror fights not only for the physical security of its citizens. It also fights for their reason to live, for their humanity, for everything that makes them human and civilised.[3]

We punish criminals for many reasons. To deter others of course, but that is not the most important reason. We punish them so the wrong done to their victims and the pain caused to those who love them is acknowledged by the community. And we also punish them because their crimes are an offence against the community whose laws are broken. With considerable eloquence Grossman shows why terrorism is an attack, not just on particular communities, but on the very conditions of humane communality. For that reason perhaps, terrorists should always be tried in an international court, or at least under a charge that makes transparent the nature of their offence against humanity. But for that to happen there has first to be much philosophical and legal thinking—jurisprudential thinking—about what terrorism is, about its different forms (including state terrorism), about what distinguishes it from other forms of political violence, justified and unjustified, and about the kinds of laws and conventions that should protect the rights of those who are suspected and convicted of it. September 11 showed the need—if it needed showing—for the further development and strengthening, of international law, but neither should be rushed for that would add to the jurisprudential confusion that mars a considerable portion of international law.

More strikingly perhaps than any other nation, the United States exhibits bewildering moral complexity. Bryan Appleyard wrote scathingly in the *Times* about the reflex anti-Americanism of much of the British intelligentsia and of its foolish condescension to a nation that boasts finer universities and finer writers than can now be found in Britain. 'I am sick', he says, 'of my generation's whining ingratitude, its wilful, infantile loathing of the great, tumultuous, witty and infinitely clever nation that has so often saved us from ourselves.' 'Of course,' he later concedes, 'there are times for criticism, lampoons, even abuse.'[4]

It's not much of a concession and, of course, Appleyard didn't intend it to be. But the United States' great virtues will not dilute the evil it has sometimes done directly and indirectly in pursuit of truly swinish policies in, for example, Central and South America.

If one thinks those virtues can dilute the evil, one will never understand why so many of the poor of the earth hate, admire and envy the United States, in a state of moral and psychic confusion potent enough to make anyone mad. And one will encourage still further the grotesque self-deception that appears to afflict many Americans and which enables them to believe that before September 11 the United States was a sleeping giant (as Edward Said put it), innocent of anything that might even partially explain (though of course not justify) why its government, but not its people, is hated in some parts of the world.[5] One hopes the sleep-walking is temporary and that, as in the days of the Vietnam War, the United States will again deliver to the world the most radical, penetrating and informed critiques of its own politics.

How much of the hatred would disappear if the United States and its allies convincingly showed its resolve to do whatever it could to ameliorate the misery caused by the injustices it committed or to which it acquiesced? No one really knows, I am sure, just as no one knows how much Palestinian hatred against Israel and Jews more generally would survive the creation of a Palestinian state alongside Israel. The apparent hatred of Israel throughout the Muslim world is a bad omen. Without any effort to disguise it, hatred of Zionism has become hatred of Jews, which—if one goes only by the rhetoric that expresses it—would not be assuaged even by the replacement of Israel with a secular state for Arabs and Jews in the whole of Palestine.

Most people acknowledge that a war that is prosecuted with reckless lack of concern for civilian causalities is unjust. More controversial is the belief that one prosecutes a war unjustly if one kills too many civilians (two for every combatant was the figure estimated in the Vietnam War), even if that is the unavoidable consequence of pursuing an enemy who has hidden 'among the people like fish in the ocean'. If, however, the distinction between civilians and combatants is to be the expression of respect for human life rather than a prudential maxim based on the fear that its breach would lead to fearful consequences, then that respect must also be shown to combatants. Observance of the distinction between the killing of combatants and the killing of civilians does not overlap neatly with the distinction between respect for human life and contempt for it.

Bomb-throwing Russian anarchists of the nineteenth century, who gave themselves up for execution after they had murdered, arguably showed a kind of respect for human life even when they deliberately killed civilians. The 'softening up' operations that bombed tens of thousands of Iraqi soldiers into the desert sands of Iraq and Kuwait, and which apparently provoked contempt for the United States in much of the Arab world, showed a brutal lack of regard for human life. It is hard to see how one could show such contempt for the humanity of combatants and at the same time show respect for the humanity of civilians by careful (and much publicised) attempts to minimise 'collateral damage'. Respect for the humanity of others is not so easily divisible. The frequent attempt to make it so is one of the reasons why George Orwell was scornful of the sometimes hypocritical importance we attach to the distinction between combatants and civilians.[6]

'Do you think our enemy will lay down its arms just because we insist on being nice!' That is how one former US general put his objection to what he regarded as the childish constraints moralists would place on the conduct of war. Crude though his expression of it was, the thought he expressed was not crude. Ever since Socrates claimed that it is better to suffer evil than to do it, the same thought has been invoked to remind us that in politics one has sometimes to decide whether one will adopt the only means available for one's defence or renounce them because they are unjust. Nothing in morality can save us from the possibility that we will face an enemy who is cunning enough to ensure that the only available means for our self-defence are evil. It is mere whistling in the dark to believe, as a distinguished Catholic moralist put it, that though morality may lead us to tragedy, it can never lead us to disaster.[7]

Socrates' affirmation (and St Paul's injunction that is often associated with it—that one may not do evil though good may come of it) is the affirmation that nothing matters so much as to live one's life decently—where nothing really means nothing. Plato understood that such a morality—call it an affirmation of absolute value—cannot inform politics. As a fine English philosopher once put it, the Socratic ethic is an ethic of forgoing and, for many reasons, forgoing is not the nature of politics.[8] Morality, as Socrates understood it, may require us to renounce the means to achieve what we most passionately and decently desire and the means to protect what we rightly cherish. But if there is anything that looks like an absolute requirement for politicians, it is that they must protect the conditions under which political communality may survive into the future. That, at any rate, is how one might characterise the perception, as old as Plato, that morality and politics may come into irreconcilable conflict.

For the defence of community, politicians will always do evil if they judge it to be necessary. Most people know that, and most people expect it of them under pain of irresponsibility. Torn between incommensurable imperatives, one political, the other moral, politicians must sometimes do what morally they must not do. To think that the conflicting imperatives must be moral imperatives if they are truly answerable to a serious conception of responsibility, is to be in the grip, I think, of a moralistic conception of responsibility. And to think that if the political imperative is genuinely an expression of responsibility then it can, and sometimes must, *justify* the actions of the politician is to fail to see fully the tragic mismatch that can exist between the world and what can justify us and our deeds. That, at any rate, is how things appear to someone who looks at our moral and political lives from the perspective of a longstanding and powerful part of the Western tradition.

Another part of the tradition, also longstanding and powerful, debunks that perspective. It assumes that the conflict that is portrayed as being between morality and politics is really a conflict within morality, and one, moreover, that can always be resolved by the creative adaptation of morality to political circumstances. This second strand of our tradition takes itself to be the only conception of morality that has thoroughly and clear-sightedly purged itself of religious commitments. If morality is of human origin, then—it is tempting but mistaken to infer—morality's purpose must be to serve human wellbeing, and sometimes it will be necessary to recast it creatively so that it can better fulfil its purpose. From this perspective, the belief that morality and the world might be tragically mismatched looks like precious and self-indulgent muddle.

There can be little doubt that this latter conception is gaining ground and that its success is a sign of the times. But that does not mean that it is a conception of morality that has been rationally adapted to the times. People often speak of morality as though it needs constant updating if it is to be adequate to the times. It is natural to think, for example, that modern weapons and modern methods of war require us to revise the doctrine of just war developed hundreds of years ago. But as I listen to arguments about this I am struck by the fact that people's sense of what is morally at issue has changed little over the centuries. The same concepts as before determine their dilemmas. It is probably true that the morality of renunciation in which just war theory is imbedded—expressed in St Paul's injunction that evil may not be done though good may come of it or great harm avoided by it—is uncongenial to the modern temper, but that is not because that morality is demonstrably inadequate to the times. Those who renounce the only means available to avert terrible consequences are not necessarily ignorant of anything, nor do they necessarily fail to appreciate fully the terrible consequences of their renunciation. There is no reason to think they could persist in their renunciation only because they are whistling in the dark, hoping for outcomes that no one aware of the facts of human life could realistically hope for.

The attack on the towers was not, I think, a watershed event. When people saw in it something new, frightening and awesome, their attention was, I believe, seized by and directed to a change that had occurred many years before and which had been noticed by (among others) many who reflected on the Australian government's recent response to the asylum seekers.

Long before September 11 many people—especially young people—felt that in the future politics will be dominated by crises that are caused and inflamed by the shameful gap between the rich and the poor nations, aggravated sometimes by ecological crises. For them, the urgent questions centre on international human rights, ecological issues and equality between nations as much as equality within them. Many of them believe, I think, that the distinction between what we have a right or an obligation to do as a sovereign nation and what we might freely do for 'humanitarian' reasons cannot survive much longer in its present form. Actions and policies that we now regard as humane but optional will become political obligations that fall upon us by virtue of our place in the community of nations. The question will be asked, 'Why merely because we are fortunate to be born in a particular location on this earth, should we enjoy wealth, health and security and be able, in the name of sovereignty, to deny it to others who, merely because they are born elsewhere, suffer the miseries and the humiliations of the damned?' It is a question that must have occurred to many Australians when they saw crack Australian troops board the *Tampa*, a ship carrying over 400 asylum seekers.

Almost childlike in its simplicity, that question will become morally unavoidable. Any serious answer to it will have radical implications. Fortress Australia was the Australian government's response when it glimpsed those implications. No one, of course, can sensibly believe that anyone should be permitted to live wherever they want to. But if we rise to the question's simple moral force, we will, I hope, rethink the relative importance we attach to an appeal to rights, on the one hand, and to our obligation to need on the other. In many poor nations the wealthy lived behind electrified razor wire. One doesn't have to be a futurologist to foresee their doom, though it remains to be seen whether those who ensure their doom will take their place behind the wire. Increasingly the defensive policies of the wealthy nations look like national versions of living behind razor wire. They try to justify it, as the Howard government tried to justify its mean-spirited response to the needs of asylum seekers, by appeal to the rights of sovereign nations.

Again and again the twentieth century forced the question on us: how could ordinary people so easily lose their humanity by failing to recognise the humanity in others? How could ordinary people come to consent to and even participate in atrocities against their fellow-citizens and even against their neighbours with whom they had previously lived closely and peaceably. Nothing gives us reason to think that we have reduced even slightly the likelihood that the same question will not be asked of us and our children.

Almost certainly our children and the generation beyond will not be protected to the degree that we have from the terrors suffered by most of the peoples of the earth, because of poverty, natural disasters and the evils inflicted upon them by other human beings. Simone Weil called the *Iliad* a miraculous document because no one could know from its accounts of the fate of the soldiers in the warring armies whether it was written by a Greek or a Trojan, so respectful is it of the humanity of both sides. No one, in my judgement, has written so hardheadedly about the almost insuperable difficulty of seeing the full humanity of those who are severely afflicted and who are degraded and humiliated in their affliction. The novelist Orhan Pamuk saw as clearly as Weil that the degradation of the afflicted was the greatest obstacle to the acknowledgement of their terrible suffering by Western governments. He wrote:

> It is neither Islam nor even poverty itself that succours terrorists, whose ferocity and creativity are unprecedented in human history, but the crushing humiliation that has infected third world countries like cancer . . . Nothing can fuel support for 'Islamists' who throw nitric acid at women because they reveal their faces as much as the West's failure to understand the damned of the world.[9]

Confrontation with the degradation that affliction and evil can visit on human beings will test our children's understanding of what it means to share a common humanity with all the peoples of the earth, and to a degree almost too awful to imagine, their faith that the world is a good world despite the suffering and the evil in it.

Many people believe that talk of evil will hinder that understanding and corrode their faith because it will harden their hearts. President Bush will do nothing to disabuse them of this. Many people also believe that serious use of the concepts presupposes religious commitment. In my judgement, none of this is necessarily true. Hannah Arendt, who was not religious nor given to simplifications, remarked that 'the men of the eighteenth century did not know that there exists goodness beyond virtue and evil beyond vice'.[10] She did not, of course, mean that 'the men of the eighteenth century' literally did not know of good and evil, or that they had no serious use for these concepts in their lives. She meant that they left no serious place for them in their political and moral philosophies.

An arresting epigram, I think, but what to make of it? Is not compassion often an expression of goodness, and is it not a virtue? Is not malevolent cruelty an evil, and is it not also a vice? The answer I would offer is that someone who affirms that every human being is infinitely precious and owed unconditional respect (or sacred, as a religious person would say) will look differently at compassion and cruelty than someone who cannot or will not do so. The former might speak of goodness in ways that invite a capital 'G' and of evil in ways that make clear that both are interdependent with that sense of preciousness. On account of that interdependence that person will think of good and evil as distinctive amongst the moral concepts, rather than merely extravagant expressions of praise in one case and condemnation in the other.

Judge the evil deed, but not the doer, we sometimes say, and rightly. But some evildoers are not even slightly remorseful, have characters as foul as their deeds, and there appears nothing in them from which remorse might grow. That is how many Americans seems to look upon fighters for al-Qaeda. On occasions—perhaps on most occasions—evil-doers might seem that way to us only because we have not seen the good in them. I doubt that it *must* be so. The belief that it must be possible for sensitive perception to discover some good in them is, I think, a counterfeit of the affirmation, unsupported by reason, that even such people are owed unconditional respect. It is dangerous to put that affirmation in the form of an empirical assessment of what awaits discovery in every evildoer for those who have eyes to see. If realism forces us to conclude that it is not always so, we are likely to succumb to the belief that there are, after all, some people who deserve to be shot in the street like mad dogs. Ironically, therefore, it is the concept of evil, interdependent with the conception of goodness that affirms that every human being is infinitely precious, that enables us to keep even the most radical evil-doers among us as our fellow human beings. The best part of our tradition has taught that evil can be understood for what it is only in the light of the kind of goodness that is most purely revealed in the works of saintly love.

There is much reason to be anxious about the way President Bush and others in his administration talk about good and evil. But their foolish and dangerous talk gives us no more reason to abandon talk of good and evil than their equally foolish and dangerous talk of infinite justice gives us reason to abandon talk of justice.

As the war proceeds, debate between left and right is becoming acrimonious. The right wishes to impose on discussion a false disjunction—either one goes in for a self-lacerating anti-war defeatism or one becomes (from the point of view of the left) a reckless supporter of military intervention in other nations. It is desperately important that we do not succumb to the illusion that realistically these are the alternatives.

Disgust with US hypocrisy should not blind us to the great difference between the United States and the kind of state al-Qaeda would wish to impose. Nor should we think that the hypocritical prosecution of the war against terror would do much to diminish that distance, the present attacks on liberty notwithstanding. US hypocrisy and the United States brutal pursuit (no one who knows the history of Central and South America could think that 'brutal' is an unjust description) of her interests in the international arena is not new. In the past it did not reduce significantly the distance between the kind of government her citizens enjoyed and the kind of governments most of her enemies endured, and it is unlikely to do so now. But that sober realisation should not tempt us to mistaken belief that to offer harsh criticism of the United States and her allies is 'objectively' to support her enemies. Nothing should relieve us of the obligation to think hard and honestly.

The capacity to make distinctions and to judge their significance is the essence of thought. Nothing can guarantee that we will be spared the fate of those wretched human beings who, as Arendt brought out in her book *Eichmann in Jerusalem*, became accomplices to, and sometimes perpetrators of, terrible crimes, on account of a kind of thoughtlessness.[11] We can be sure, though, that we will be lost if we yield to impatience and mock the fine distinctions that we will need to draw if we are to give answers that are both intelligent and decent to the questions: What response to evil is justified? What is justified in war?

During the period when I wrote the first draft of this essay, I was teaching a seminar on Plato's *Gorgias* in London, amid warnings that London was likely to be the next target for massive terrorist attacks. The *Gorgias* is the dialogue in which Socrates announces his faith that it is better to suffer evil than to do it. This provokes incredulity and ridicule on the part of his interlocutors, one of whom says rightly enough that, 'If what you say is true Socrates, then the whole of human life is turned upside down'.

None of the students failed to see the relevance of the exchange between Socrates and his interlocutors to their thoughts about our present situation, about what it might require of us morally. Wonderfully, none of them doubted that there is much to be learnt from this text written two and a half thousand years ago. None of them thought that the passage of time has shown its lessons to be naive or dated, or diminished its authority to call us to a serious questioning of ourselves and what we take for granted. Foolish though it may seem, in these dark times I find that enormously heartening.

Notes

1 Toward a Definition of Terrorism

1 This is an edited version of an address given to the Australian Institute of Polish Affairs dinner, Mercure Hotel, Melbourne, 3 November 2001.
2 Laqueur, *The Age of Terrorism*, p. 309.
3 Laqueur, *The Age of Terrorism*, p. 21, and O'Sullivan, *Terrorism, Ideology and Revolution*, p. 213.

2 Terrorism, Just War and Supreme Emergency

1 Schmid, *Political Terrorism*, pp. 119–58, cited in Laqueur, *The Age of Terrorism*, p. 143.
2 Terrorism Research Center Inc., viewed 17 June 2002, <http://www.terrorism.com/terrorism/def.shtml>.
3 Arafat, 'The Palestinian Vision of Peace', p. 15.
4 Yeager, *Yeager*, pp. 89–90.
5 Locke, *Second Treatise of Civil Government*, p. 435.
6 See Holmes, *On War and Morality*, pp. 193–203.
7 Walzer, *Just and Unjust Wars*, ch. 16; and Rawls, *Collected Papers*, pp. 565–72.
8 This is not the place for a full discussion of this complex tradition, but I have discussed it elsewhere. See Coady, 'Messy Morality and the Art of the Possible'; 'Dirty Hands', in Singer (ed.), *A Companion to Ethics*; Coady, 'Dirty Hands', in L. and C. Becker (eds), *The Encyclopedia of Ethics*; and Coady, 'Dirty Hands and Politics', in Goodin and Pettit (eds), *A Companion to Contemporary Political Philosophy*. For Walzer's influential statement of the position see his 'Political Action: The Problem of Dirty Hands'.
9 Walzer, *Just and Unjust Wars*, p. 260.
10 Walzer, *Just and Unjust Wars*, pp. 267–68.
11 See, for instance, Chang, *The Rape of Nanking*, pp. 4–6.
12 See Sartre, *No Exit and Three Other Plays*.
13 Walzer, *Just and Unjust Wars*, p. 254.
14 Wittgenstein, *On Certainty*, and Quine, 'Two Dogmas of Empiricism', pp. 20–43.
15 Walzer, *Just and Unjust Wars*, p. 254. At least this seems to be what he is saying. The issue is confused by his tendency here, as elsewhere, to put the point as though he is reporting common opinion: 'it is not usually said of individuals in

domestic society that they necessarily will or that they morally can strike out at innocent people, even in the supreme emergency of self-defense. They can only attack their attackers'.

[16] Walzer, *Just and Unjust Wars*, p. 254.

3 *Political Terrorism as a Weapon of the Politically Powerless*

[1] Primoratz, ch. 4 in this volume.

[2] *Pace* Teichman, *Pacifism and the Just War*, p. 92; and Igor Primoratz, 'What Is Terrorism?' (1990), pp. 133 ff.

[3] Wardlaw, *Political Terrorism*, p. 42.

[4] Wilkinson, *Political Terrorism*; Coady, 'The Morality of Terrorism'; Walzer, 'Terrorism'; Primoratz, 'What Is Terrorism?'; Lomasky, 'The Political Significance of Terrorism'.

[5] Coady, 'The Morality of Terrorism', p. 52.

[6] Primoratz, 'What Is Terrorism?', p. 133.

[7] Primoratz, 'What Is Terrorism?', p. 136.

[8] For example, see my 'Revolutionary Terrorism, Crime and Morality'; and Valls, 'Can Terrorism Be Justified?'

[9] Walzer, 'Terrorism', p. 239.

[10] As cited in Held, 'Terrorism, Rights, and Political Goals', p. 78.

[11] Walzer, 'Terrorism: A Critique of Excuses', p. 240.

[12] Jan Narveson, 'Terrorism and Morality', p. 14, relying on Edward Hyams, *Terrorists and Terrorism*. For helpful discussion of one element of the terrorism in Northern Ireland in the past century see George, 'The Ethics of IRA Terrorism'.

[13] Robert Fullinwider has drawn attention to the way that terrorism has sometimes been used within what are considered democracies to achieve *industrial* (as against *political*) change. See his 'Understanding Terrorism', pp. 252 ff.

[14] For helpful discussion see Gordon and Lopez, 'Terrorism in the Arab–Israeli Conflict'.

[15] See, for example, Walzer, *Just and Unjust Wars*; Johnson, *Just War Tradition and the Restraint of War*; Holmes, *On War and Morality*.

[16] For an introduction to the issues raised by these remarks see, for example, Kagan, *Normative Ethics*.

[17] For example, Hare, 'On Terrorism'.

4 *State Terrorism*

[1] Woddis, 'Ethics for Everyman', quoted in Coady, 'The Morality of Terrorism', p. 52.

[2] Laqueur, *The Age of Terrorism*, p. 146. In his latest book, *The New Terrorism*, Laqueur remains faithful to this approach. The book includes a chapter on 'State Terrorism', but its scope is clearly circumscribed in its first sentence: 'State-*sponsored* terrorism, warfare by proxy, is as old as the history of military conflict' (p. 156, emphasis added). State terrorism in the strict sense is still beyond Laqueur's ken: 'Terrorism seldom appeared in brutal dictatorships such as Nazi Germany or Stalinist Russia, for the simple reason that repression in these regimes made it impossible for the terrorists to organize' (p. 6).

[3] For a sample of social science research illustrating a different approach, see Stohl and Lopez, *The State as Terrorist*.

[4] See Glover, 'State Terrorism'; Ryan, 'State and Private; Red and White'; Gilbert, *Terrorism, Security and Nationality*, ch. 9; Ashmore, 'State Terrorism and Its Sponsors'.

[5] See my 'What Is Terrorism?', and 'The Morality of Terrorism', pp. 221–2.

[6] I believe that the mainstream understanding of 'the innocent' is too generous, but for present purposes this issue is best put to one side. See my 'Michael Walzer's Just War Theory: Some Issues of Responsibility'.

[7] Ryan, 'State and Private; Red and White', p. 249.

[8] Friedrich and Brzezinski, *Totalitarian Dictatorship and Democracy*, pp. 169–70.

[9] Laqueur, *The Age of Terrorism*, p. 146.

[10] Rushdie, 'How to Defeat Terrorism'.

[11] See Middlebrook, *The Battle of Hamburg*, ch. 15.

[12] Kolnai, 'Erroneous Conscience', pp. 14–22.

[13] See my 'The Morality of Terrorism'.

[14] See Walzer, *Just and Unjust Wars*, ch. 16. For a good discussion of the moral issues involved in the RAF terror bombing of Germany, see Garrett, *Ethics and Airpower in World War II*.

[15] Walzer, *Just and Unjust Wars*, p. 261.

[16] See Cigar, *Genocide in Bosnia*, ch. 5.

[17] See Kavka, 'Some Paradoxes of Deterrence'.

[18] This is a revised and expanded version of a paper read at the Austrian Ludwig Wittgenstein Society conference on applied ethics held in August 1998 in Kirchberg am Wechsel, Austria, and printed in the conference proceedings.

5 *Osama bin Laden, Terrorism and Collective Responsibility*

[1] Bergen, *Holy War Inc*, ch. 3.

[2] Abagiah, 'Shaking the Foundations', p. 37.

[3] Hanrahan, 'America the Unloved', p. 47.

[4] See Saeed, ch. 7 in this volume.

[5] As Chomsky points out, Nicaragua took the United States to the World Court in relation to US attacks on Nicaragua in the 1980s. The World Court ruled in Nicaragua's favour ordering the United States to desist and pay reparations. The United States refused to do so, despite having been found to have contravened international law by the World Court. According to Chomsky, this was the United States deploying terrorism. See Chomsky, *September 11*, p. 25.

[6] Bergen, *Holy War Inc*.

[7] Bergen, *Holy War Inc*, ch. 3.

[8] Wilkins, *Terrorism and Collective Responsibility*, p. 26.

[9] Quoted in Bergen, *Holy War Inc*, p. 105.

[10] Huntington, *The Clash of Civilisations and the Remaking of World Order*.

[11] Cooper, 'Collective Responsibility, "Moral Luck" and Reconciliation'.

[12] French, *Collective and Corporate Responsibility*.

[13] Wilkins, *Terrorism and Collective Responsibility*.

[14] Miller, *Social Action*, ch. 5.

[15] Miller, *Social Action*, ch. 8.

[16] Miller, *Social Action*, ch. 2.

[17] I am not claiming that being a beneficiary of wrongdoing never warrants retaliation on the part of those wronged.

[18] See Miller, *Social Action*, ch. 8.

[19] See Miller, *Social Action*, ch. 8.

6 Towards Liberation

1 See Young, ch. 3 in this volume.
2 In his collection of essays, *The Wretched of the Earth*. Jean-Paul Sartre has provided a rather succinct but useful commentary on the essay in the preface he wrote to this edition.
3 Osama bin Laden, videotaped statement of 7 October 2001, Associated Press translation from Arabic, viewed 3 April 2002, <http://users.skynet.be/terrorism/html/laden_statement.htm>. The BBC translation differs from the above at a few important points. For example, 'oppression' is translated as 'falsehood'. See <http://news.bbc.co.uk/hi/english/world/south_asia/newsid_1585000/1585636.stm>, viewed 3 April 2002.
4 Al-Qaeda spokesman seems to refer to this difference. See <http://news.bbc.co.uk/hi/e. . ./middle_east/newsid_1590000/1590350.stm>, viewed 3 April 2002.
5 Fanon explicitly argues that violence is 'cleansing' in this way. See *The Wretched of the Earth*, p. 74.
6 In ch. 3 of this volume, Robert Young examines this type of justification as a form of consequentialist justification of terrorism.
7 To validate this inference one needs to introduce further premises or assumptions that are not of central interest for our present inquiry. Of course, not all of those who accept (a) are ready to make the inference to (b) and (c).
8 In his preface, referred to in note 2.

7 Jihad and Violence

1 Abd al-Hakim, 'War and Peace'; Siddiqi, 'Jihad, an Instrument of Islamic Revolution'; Johnson and Kelsay, *Cross, Crescent and Sword*; Khadduri, *War and Peace in the Law of Islam*; Jansen, *The Neglected Duty*; Peters, *Jihad in Classical and Modern Islam*.
2 Lane, *Arabic–English Lexicon*, p. 473.
3 Qur'an 2:218; 8:72; 9:20.
4 Qur'an 9:20, 88.
5 This can be seen in the section on jihad in most legal texts. See for instance, Ibn Rushd, *The Distinguished Jurist's Primer*.
6 Qur'an 2:39–40.
7 Qur'an 9:13.
8 Qur'an 2:190–4; 4:90–1; 4:84; 9:12–13; 9:36.
9 Qur'an 9:4.
10 For this see Qur'an, Surah 9.
11 For further details see Qutb, 'War, Peace, and Islamic Jihad', pp. 224–5.
12 For a discussion of various categories of people the Prophet had to deal with and how they were to be treated, see Qutb, 'War, Peace, and Islamic Jihad', pp. 224–5.
13 Johnson, *The Holy War Idea in Western and Islamic Traditions*, p. 157.
14 These three worlds refer to *dar al-islam, dar al-sulh* and *dar al-kufr*, respectively.
15 Johnson, *The Holy War Idea in Western and Islamic Traditions*, pp. 146–7.
16 See, for example, Ibn Rushd, *The Distinguished Jurist's Primer*, p. 464.
17 However, some Muslim jurists argue that jihad can be waged against specific categories of non-Muslims 'for their conversion to Islam or the payment of *jizya* (a tax imposed on non-Muslims under the protection of Muslim rule)'. See Ibn Rushd, *The Distinguished Jurist's Primer*, p. 464.

[18] Qur'an 2:256.
[19] Ibn Rushd, *The Distinguished Jurist's Primer*, pp. 461–2.
[20] Ibn Rushd, *The Distinguished Jurist's Primer*, p. 458.
[21] Malik b. Anas, *Al-Muwatta of Imam Malik ibn Anas*, p. 174.
[22] Ibn Rushd, *The Distinguished Jurist's Primer*, vol. 1, p. 460.
[23] Ibn Rushd, *The Distinguished Jurist's Primer*, vol. 1, p. 456.
[24] Peters, *Jihad in Classical and Modern Islam*, pp. 104–5.
[25] Moulavi Chiragh Ali, 'War and Peace: Popular Jihad', p. 71.
[26] Peters, *Jihad in Classical and Modern Islam*, p. 6.
[27] Peters, *Jihad in Classical and Modern Islam*, p. 6.
[28] Peters, *Jihad in Classical and Modern Islam*, p. 6.
[29] Peters, *Jihad in Classical and Modern Islam*, p. 6.
[30] Abul A'la Maududi, *Jihad in Islam*, p. 5.
[31] Qutb, 'War, Peace, and Islamic Jihad', pp. 223–45.

8 Terrorism and the Right to Wage War

[1] Primoratz, 'What Is Terrorism?', p. 129.
[2] Coady, 'The Morality of Terrorism', p. 52.
[3] Coady, 'The Morality of Terrorism', p. 62.
[4] Coates, *The Ethics of War*, p. 124.
[5] Coady, 'The Morality of Terrorism', p. 52.
[6] Young, in this volume.
[7] Coates, *The Ethics of War*, p. 123.
[8] Coates, *The Ethics of War*, p. 127.
[9] Coates, *The Ethics of War*, pp. 126–7.
[10] For example, in Coates, *The Ethics of War*, ch. 6.
[11] On the other hand, during the war German soldiers were treated according to war conventions and not as people engaged in a criminal conspiracy. This treatment could be justified by a reasonable distinction between a people and its leaders. The German government had to be removed, but the German nation would have a continued existence, and the treatment of Germans had to reflect a respect for their eventual right to take their place in world society.

9 Responding Justly to International Terrorism

[1] Tony Coady and Igor Primoratz deserve thanks for their comments on an earlier draft of this chapter.
[2] See the analysis of definitions of terrorism in Coady's chapter in this volume. See also the debate in the Organisation of Islamic Conference on terrorism in April 2002, *Australian*, 4 April 2002, p. 8.
[3] Laqueur, *The New Terrorism*, pp. 5–6 (he also cites the US Department of Defense definition); Poland, *Understanding Terrorism*, pp. 9–10; Lodge, *Terrorism*, p. 5; Coady, 'The Morality of Terrorism', pp. 51–2.
[4] See Primoratz's chapter in this volume.
[5] Some of these broader issues are dealt with by Crenshaw, 'The Causes of Terrorism', and Walzer, 'The Moral Standing of States'.
[6] See, for instance, Regan, *Just War*, pp. 17–18, and Coady, 'The Immunity of Combatants'.

⁷ This construction avoids the issue of whether non-combatants are 'innocent'. See Coates, *The Ethics of War*, pp. 234–72.

⁸ Regan, *Just War*, pp. 88–9, and O'Brien, *The Conduct of Just and Limited Wars*, pp. 44–7, 338–41. Some strategists never recognised the distinction in war, see Liddell Hart, *The Current of War*, pp. 54–5.

⁹ See Primoratz's chapter in this volume, and Walzer, *Just and Unjust Wars*, ch. 9.

¹⁰ See Fullinwider, 'War and Innocence', and Wilkins, *Terrorism and Collective Responsibility*, ch. 4.

¹¹ Rapoport, 'The Politics of Atrocity', p. 47.

¹² See Aquinas, *Summa Theologiae*, II–II, Q. 64, A. 6.

¹³ See Phillips, 'Combatancy, Noncombatancy, and Noncombatant Immunity in Just War Tradition'.

¹⁴ See Young's chapter in this volume, and Paskins and Dockrill, *The Ethics of War*, p. 254.

¹⁵ von Clausewitz, *On War*, pp. 119–20.

¹⁶ See for instance, Department of Defence, *The Defence of Australia 1987*, pp. 23–6, and Department of Defence, *Strategic Review 1993*, p. 43.

¹⁷ Terrorism is often attributed to injustices, and therefore ameliorating these problems is a strategy that should go hand in hand with traditional military conceptions of counterterrorism. See Young, ch. 3 in this volume.

¹⁸ Wilkinson, *Political Terrorism*, pp. 136–42.

¹⁹ See Alexander, Brown and Nanes (eds), *Control of Terrorism*, and Murphy, *Punishing International Terrorists*.

²⁰ The legal term is *aut dedere aut punire*.

²¹ Article 42 of the Charter reserves the right for the Security Council to take offensive military action when international peace and security is threatened.

²² Article 51 of the UN Charter discusses the principle of self-defence, but it is not treated as a license to mount unilateral operations; see Regan, *Just War*, pp. 53–6.

²³ See Young, ch. 3 in this volume. See also Quinton, 'Terrorism and Political Violence', pp. 55–6, and Paskins and Dockrill, *The Ethics of War*, pp. 88, 90, 94.

²⁴ For a discussion of terrorism in this context see Kelsay, *Islam and War*, especially chs 4 and 5. See also Capitanchik, 'Terrorism and Islam', and Saeed's chapter in this volume.

²⁵ See Walzer, 'Terrorism: A Critique of Excuses', p. 239.

²⁶ See Paskins and Dockrill, *The Ethics of War*, pp. 86–9.

²⁷ See, for instance, Dror, 'Challenge to the Democratic Capacity to Govern'.

²⁸ This chapter is only concerned with responses to terrorism in the international arena, so limiting civil liberties is beyond its purview.

²⁹ Johnson, *Just War Tradition and the Restraint of War*, p. 50.

³⁰ Australian Federated Press, 'Congress Allocates More Bribery Money', p. 7.

³¹ See, for instance, McGrory and Fletcher, 'Bush Works Overtime to Break EU Deadlock on Jailed Terrorists'.

³² See Albrechtsen, 'Soldiers of Terror Don't Have Rights', and the overview in Poland, *Understanding Terrorism*, pp. 5–7. For a counterview, see Gerstein, 'Do Terrorists Have Rights?'

³³ Walzer, *Just and Unjust Wars*, pp. 251–5. See also Coady, ch. 2 in this volume.

³⁴ Keal, *Ethics and Foreign Policy*, p. 29.

³⁵ See Coates, *The Ethics of War*, pp. 123–45, and Thompson, ch. 8 in this volume.

[36] Osama bin Laden broadcast a declaration of war on the Qatar-based al-Jazeera television network.

[37] See Lieber, 'Guerrilla Parties Considered with Reference to the Laws and Usages of War', pp. 33–4.

[38] Article 4 of the 1949 Geneva Convention affords places obligations on states when they capture enemy soldiers. These prisoners of war gain these rights because they can be clearly identified by wearing insignia, carry weapons openly, and follow the law of war (conduct of war). For a discussion of moral equivalence see Walzer, *Just and Unjust Wars*, pp. 34–7.

[39] Wilkinson, 'Fighting the Hydra', p. 222.

[40] See Falk, 'Means and Ends in the Struggle Against Global Terrorism', p. 53.

10 *A 'War of Good Against Evil'*

[1] Aeschylus, *The Libation Bearers*.

[2] Margalit, 'The Middle East: Snakes and Ladders'.

[3] Grossman, 'Terror's Long Shadow'.

[4] Appleyard, 'Why Do They Hate America?', p. 1.

[5] Said, 'The Events and Aftermath', *Observer*, viewed 16 September 2001, <http://www.zmag.org/saidcalam.htm>.

[6] Orwell, *Collected Essays, Journalism and Letters of George Orwell*, vol. 3, pp. 179–80.

[7] Donagan, *The Theory of Morality*, p. 206.

[8] Holland, *Against Empiricism*, pp. 126–42.

[9] Pamuk, 'Listen to the Damned'.

[10] Arendt, *On Revolution*, pp. 81–2.

[11] Arendt, *Eichmann in Jerusalem*.

Bibliography

Abagiah, George, 'Shaking the Foundations', in J. Baxter and M. Downing (eds), *The Day That Shook the World*, ABC Books, Sydney, 2001, pp. 35–44.

Abd al-Hakim, Khalifa, 'War and Peace', in A. Ahmad and G. von Grunebaum (eds), *Muslim Self-statement in India and Pakistan, 1858–1968*, Harrassowitz, Wiesbaden, 1970, pp. 182–9.

Aeschylus, *The Libation Bearers*, trans. by Hugh Lloyd-Jones, intro. by Eric A. Havelock, Prentice-Hall, Englewood Cliffs, NJ, 1970.

Albrechtsen, Janet, 'Soldiers of Terror Don't Have Rights', *Australian*, 13 February 2002, p. 11.

Alexander, Yonah, Brown, Marjorie and Nanes, Allen (eds), *Control of Terrorism: International Documents*, Crane, New York, 1978.

Ali, Moulavi Chiragh, 'War and Peace: Popular Jihad', in M. Moaddel and K. Talattof (eds), *Contemporary Debates in Islam*, Macmillan, London, 2000, pp. 71–94.

Appleyard, Bryan, 'Why Do They Hate America?', *Sunday Times, News Review*, 23 September 2001, p. 1.

Aquinas, Thomas Saint, *Summa Theologiae: Latin Text and English Translation, Introductions, Notes, Appendices, and Glossaries*, Blackfriars, Cambridge; McGraw-Hill, New York, 1964–81.

Arafat, Yasser, 'The Palestinian Vision of Peace', *New York Times*, 3 February 2002, p. 15.

Arendt, Hannah, *Eichmann in Jerusalem: A Report on the Banality of Evil*, Viking, New York, 1964.

——, *On Revolution*, Viking, New York, 1973.

Ashmore, R. B., 'State Terrorism and Its Sponsors', in T. Kapitan (ed.), *Philosophical Perspectives on the Israeli-Palestinian Conflict*, M. E. Sharpe, Armonk, NY, 1997, pp. 105–32.

Australian Federated Press, 'Congress Allocates More Bribery Money', *Australian*, 18 December 2001, p. 7.

Bergen, Peter L., *Holy War Inc: Inside the Secret World of Osama bin Laden*, Weidenfeld & Nicolson, London, 2001.

Capitanchik, David and Eichenberg, Richard C., 'Terrorism and Islam', in N. O'Sullivan (ed.), *Terrorism, Ideology and Revolution*, Wheatsheaf, Brighton, Sussex, 1986, pp. 115–32.

Chang, Iris, *The Rape of Nanking: The Forgotten Holocaust of World War II*, Penguin, Ringwood, Vic., 1998.

Chomsky, Noam, *September 11*, Allen & Unwin, Sydney, 2001.

Cigar, N., *Genocide in Bosnia: The Policy of 'Ethnic Cleansing'*, Texas A&M University Press, College Station, Tex., 1995.

Clausewitz, Carl von, *On War*, ed. by A. Rapaport, Penguin, Harmondsworth, 1982.

Coady, C. A. J. (Tony), 'The Morality of Terrorism', *Philosophy*, vol. 60, 1985, pp. 47–69.

——, 'Messy Morality and the Art of the Possible', *Aristotelian Society*, vol. 64, 1990, pp. 259–79.

——, 'Dirty Hands', in Peter Singer (ed.), *A Companion to Ethics*, Blackwell, Oxford, 1993, pp. 373–84.

——, 'Dirty Hands and Politics', in R. Goodin and P. Pettit (eds), *A Companion to Contemporary Political Philosophy*, Blackwell, Oxford, 1993, pp. 422–30.

——, 'The Immunity of Combatants', in A. Alexandra, M. Collingridge and S. Miller (eds), *The Proceedings of the Third Annual Conference of the Australian Association for Professional and Applied Ethics*, AAPAE and Charles Sturt University, Wagga Wagga, NSW, 1996, pp. 224–59.

——, 'Dirty Hands', in L. and C. Becker (eds), *The Encyclopedia of Ethics*, 2nd edn, Routledge, London, 2001, pp. 1241–4.

Coates, A. J., *The Ethics of War*, Manchester University Press, Manchester, 1997.

Cooper, David, 'Collective Responsibility, "Moral Luck" and Reconciliation', in A. Jokic (ed.), *War Crimes and Collective Wrongdoing*, Blackwell, Oxford, 2001.

Crenshaw, Martha, 'The Causes of Terrorism', *Comparative Politics*, vol. 13, no. 4, 1981, pp. 379–401.

Department of Defence, *The Defence of Australia 1987*, Australian Government Publishing Service, Canberra, 1987.

——, *Strategic Review 1993*, Australian Government Publishing Service, Canberra, 1993.

Diplomatic Conference for the Establishment of International Conventions for the Protection of Victims of War (1949, Geneva, Switzerland), *The Geneva Conventions of August 12, 1949*, International Committee of the Red Cross, Geneva, 1949.

Donagan, Alan, *The Theory of Morality*, University of Chicago Press, Chicago, 1977.

Dror, Yehezkel, 'Challenge to the Democratic Capacity to Govern', in M. Crenshaw (ed.), *Terrorism, Legitimacy and Power: The Consequences of Political Violence*, Wesleyan University Press, Middletown, Conn., 1984, pp. 65–90.

Falk, Richard, 'Means and Ends in the Struggle Against Global Terrorism', *Pacifica Review*, vol. 14, no. 1, 2002, pp. 49–56.

Fanon, Frantz, *The Wretched of the Earth*, trans. by Constance Farrington, Penguin, Harmondsworth, 1963.

French, Peter, *Collective and Corporate Responsibility*, Columbia University Press, New York, 1984.

Friedrich, C. J. and Brzezinski, Z. K., *Totalitarian Dictatorship and Democracy*, 2nd edn, Harvard University Press, Cambridge, Mass., 1965.

Fullinwider, Robert, 'Understanding Terrorism', in S. Luper-Foy (ed.), *Problems of International Justice*, Westview Press, Boulder, Colo., 1988, pp. 248–59.

——, 'War and Innocence', in C. Beitz (ed.), *International Ethics: A Philosophy and Public Affairs Reader*, Princeton University Press, Princeton, NJ, 1990, pp. 90–8.

Garrett, S. A., *Ethics and Airpower in World War II: The British Bombing of German Cities*, St Martin's Press, New York, 1993.

George, David, 'The Ethics of IRA Terrorism', in A. Valls (ed.), *Ethics in International Affairs*, Rowman & Littlefield, Lanham, Md, 2000, pp. 81–97.

Gerstein, Robert, 'Do Terrorists Have Rights?', in D. Rapoport and Y. Alexander (eds), *The Morality of Terrorism: Religious and Secular Justifications*, Pergamon, New York, 1982, pp. 290–305.

Gilbert, P., *Terrorism, Security and Nationality*, Routledge, London, 1994.

Glover, J., 'State Terrorism', in R. Frey and C. Morris (eds), *Violence, Terrorism and Justice*, Cambridge University Press, Cambridge, 1991, pp. 256–75.

Gordon, Neve and Lopez, George A., 'Terrorism in the Arab–Israeli Conflict', in A. Valls (ed.), *Ethics in International Affairs*, Rowman & Littlefield, Lanham, Md, 2000, pp. 99–113.

Grossman, David, 'Terror's Long Shadow', *Guardian, Special Report: Terrorism in the US*, viewed 21 September 2001, <http://www.guardian.co.uk/wtccrash/story/0,1300,555461,00.html>.

Hanrahan, Brian, 'America the Unloved', in J. Baxter and M. Downing (eds), *The Day That Shook the World*, ABC Books, Sydney, 2001, pp. 45–53.

Hare, R. M., 'On Terrorism', *Journal of Value Inquiry*, vol. 13, 1979, pp. 241–9.

Held, Virginia, 'Terrorism, Rights, and Political Goals', in R. Frey and C. Morris (eds), *Violence, Terrorism and Justice*, Cambridge University Press, New York, 1991, pp. 59–85.

Holland, R. F., *Against Empiricism*, Blackwell, Oxford, 1980.

Holmes, Robert L., *On War and Morality*, Princeton University Press, Princeton, NJ, 1989.

Huntington, Samuel P., *The Clash of Civilisations and the Remaking of World Order*, Simon & Schuster, New York, 1998.

Hyams, Edward, *Terrorists and Terrorism*, Dent, London, 1975.

Ibn Rushd, *The Distinguished Jurist's Primer*, vol. 1, trans. by Imran Ahsan Khan Nyazee, Garnet, Reading, 1994.

Jansen, Johannes J. G., *The Neglected Duty: The Creed of Sadat's Assassins and Islamic Resurgence in the Middle East*, Macmillan, New York, 1986.

Johnson, James T., *Just War Tradition and the Restraint of War: A Moral and Historical Inquiry*, Princeton University Press, Princeton, NJ, 1981.

——, *The Holy War Idea in Western and Islamic Traditions*, Pennsylvania State University Press, University Park, Pa, 1997.

Johnson, James T. and Kelsay, J. (eds), *Cross, Crescent and Sword: The Justification and Limitation of War in Western and Islamic Tradition*, Greenwood Press, New York, 1990.

Kagan, Shelly, *Normative Ethics*, Westview Press, Boulder, Colo., 1998.

Kavka, G. S., 'Some Paradoxes of Deterrence', *Journal of Philosophy*, vol. 75, 1978, pp. 285–302.

Keal, P. (ed.), *Ethics and Foreign Policy*, Allen & Unwin, Sydney, 1992.

Kelsay, John, *Islam and War: A Study in Comparative Ethics*, Westminster/ John Know Press, Louisville, Ky, 1993.

Khadduri, Majid, *War and Peace in the Law of Islam*, John Hopkins Press, Baltimore, Md, 1955.

Kolnai, A., 'Erroneous Conscience', in D. Wiggins and B. A. O. Williams (eds), *Ethics, Value and Reality: Selected Papers of Aurel Kolnai*, Athlone Press, London, 1977.

Lane, Edward William, *Arabic–English Lexicon*, Librairie du Liban, Beirut, 1968.

Laqueur, Walter, *The Age of Terrorism*, Little, Brown & Co., Boston, 1987.

——, *The New Terrorism: Fanaticism and the Arms of Mass Destruction*, Oxford University Press, Oxford, 1999.

Liddell Hart, B. H. , *The Current of War*, Hutchinson & Co., London, 1941.

Lieber, Francis, 'Guerrilla Parties Considered with Reference to the Laws and Usages of War', in R. Hartigan (ed.), *Lieber's Code and the Law of War*, Precedent, Chicago, 1983.

Locke, John, *Second Treatise of Civil Government*, ed. and introduced by J. W. Gough, Blackwell, Oxford, 1946.

Lodge, James (ed.), *Terrorism: A Challenge to the State*, Martin Robinson, Oxford, 1981.

Lomasky, Loren, 'The Political Significance of Terrorism', in R. Frey and C. Morris (eds), *Violence, Terrorism and Justice*, Cambridge University Press, New York, 1991, pp. 86–115.

McGrory, Daniel and Fletcher, Martin, 'Bush Works Overtime to Break EU Deadlock on Jailed Terrorists', *Australian*, 29 November 2001, p. 6.

Malik ibn Anas, *Al-Muwatta of Imam Malik ibn Anas*, trans. by Aisha Abdur-rahman Bewley, Madinah Press, Granada, 1997.

Margalit, Avishai, 'The Middle East: Snakes and Ladders', *The New York Review of Books*, viewed 17 May 2001, <http://www.nybooks.com/articles/14224>.

Maududi, Abul A'la Sayyid, *Jihad in Islam*, International Islamic Federation as Student Organisation (IIFSO), Kuwait, n.d.

Middlebrook, M., *The Battle of Hamburg*, Penguin, Harmondsworth, 1984.

Miller, Seumas, *Social Action: A Teleological Account*, Cambridge University Press, Cambridge, 2002.

Murphy, John, *Punishing International Terrorists: The Legal Framework for Policy Initiatives*, Rowman & Littlefield, Lanham, Md, 1985.

Narveson, Jan, 'Terrorism and Morality', in R. Frey and C. Morris (eds), *Violence, Terrorism and Justice*, Cambridge University Press, New York, 1991, pp. 116–69.

O'Brien, William, *The Conduct of Just and Limited Wars*, Praeger, New York, 1981.

Orwell, George, *The Collected Essays, Journalism and Letters of George Orwell*, Sonia Orwell and Ian Angus (eds), Penguin, Harmondsworth, 1968.

Pamuk, Orhan, 'Listen to the Damned', *Guardian*, viewed 29 September 2001, <http://www.guardian.co.uk/afghanistan/story/0,1284,560193,00.html>.

Paskins, Barrie and Dockrill, Michael, *The Ethics of War*, Duckworth, London, 1979.

Peters, Rudolph, *Jihad in Classical and Modern Islam*, Markus Wiener Publishers, Princeton, NJ, 1996.

Phillips, Robert, 'Combatancy, Noncombatancy, and Noncombatant Immunity in Just War Tradition', in J. Johnson and J. Kelsay (eds), *Cross, Crescent, and Sword: The Justification and Limitation of War in Western and Islamic Tradition*, Greenwood Press, New York, 1990, pp. 179–96.

Poland, James M., *Understanding Terrorism: Groups, Strategies, and Responses*, Prentice Hall, Englewood Cliffs, NJ, 1988.

Primoratz, Igor, 'What Is Terrorism?', *Journal of Applied Philosophy*, vol. 7, 1990, pp. 129–38.

——, 'The Morality of Terrorism', *Journal of Applied Philosophy*, vol. 14, no. 3, 1997, pp. 221–33.

——, 'Michael Walzer's Just War Theory: Some Issues of Responsibility', *Ethical Theory and Moral Practice*, vol. 5, 2002, pp. 221–43.

Quinton, Anthony, 'Terrorism and Political Violence: A Permanent Challenge to Governments', in M. Crenshaw (ed.), *Terrorism, Legitimacy and Power: The Consequences of Political Violence*, Wesleyan University Press, Middletown, Conn., 1984, pp. 52–64.

Quine, W. V., 'Two Dogmas of Empiricism', *Philosophical Review*, vol. 60, 1950, pp. 20–43.

Qutb, Sayyid, 'War, Peace, and Islamic Jihad', in M. Moaddel and K. Talattof (eds), *Contemporary Debates in Islam: An Anthology of Modernist and Fundamentalist Thought*, St Martin's Press, New York, 2000, pp. 223–46.

Rapoport, David, 'The Politics of Atrocity', in Y. Alexander and S. Finger (eds), *Terrorism: Interdisciplinary Perspectives*, John Jay, New York, 1977, pp. 46–61.

Rawls, John, *Collected Papers*, ed. by S. Freeman, Harvard University Press, Cambridge, Mass., 1999.

Regan, Richard, *Just War: Principles and Cases*, Catholic University of America Press, Washington, DC, 1996.

Rushdie, S., 'How to Defeat Terrorism', *Age*, 4 October 2001, p. 15.

Ryan, A., 'State and Private; Red and White', in R. Frey and C. Morris (eds), *Violence, Terrorism and Justice*, Cambridge University Press, Cambridge, 1991, pp. 230–56.

Said, Edward, 'The Events and Aftermath', *Observer*, viewed 16 September 2001, <http://www.zmag.org/saidcalam.htm>.

Sartre, Jean-Paul, *No Exit and Three Other Plays*, Vintage, New York, 1955.

Schmid, Alex Peter, *Political Terrorism: A Research Guide to Concepts, Theories, Data Bases, and Literature*, North-Holland, Amsterdam, 1983.

Siddiqi, Aslam, 'Jihad, an Instrument of Islamic Revolution', *Islamic Studies*, vol. 2, 1963, pp. 383–98.

Stohl, M. and Lopez, G. A. (eds), *The State as Terrorist: The Dynamics of Governmental Violence and Repression*, Greenwood Press, Westport, Conn., 1984.

Teichman, J., *Pacifism and the Just War*, Blackwell, Oxford, 1986.

Terrorism Research Center Inc., 'Definitions', viewed 17 June 2002, <http://www.terrorism.com/terrorism/def.shtml>.

Valls, Andrew, 'Can Terrorism Be Justified?', in A. Valls (ed.), *Ethics in International Affairs*, Rowman & Littlefield, Lanham, Md, 2000, pp. 65–79.

Walzer, Michael, 'Political Action: The Problem of Dirty Hands', *Philosophy and Public Affairs*, vol. 2, 1973, pp. 160–80.

——, *Just and Unjust Wars: A Moral Argument with Historical Illustrations*, 3rd edn, Basic Books, New York, 2000.

——, 'Terrorism: A Critique of Excuses', in S. Luper-Foy (ed.), *Problems of International Justice*, Westview Press, Boulder, Colo., 1988, pp. 237–47.

——, 'The Moral Standing of States: A Response to Four Critics', in C. Beitz (ed.), *International Ethics: A Philosophy and Public Affairs Reader*, Princeton University Press, Princeton, NJ, 1990, pp. 217–37.

Wardlaw, Grant, *Political Terrorism*, 2nd edn, Cambridge University Press, Cambridge, 1989.

Wilkins, Burleigh Taylor, *Terrorism and Collective Responsibility*, Routledge, London, 1992.

Wilkinson, Paul, *Political Terrorism*, Macmillan, London, 1974.

——, 'Fighting the Hydra: International Terrorism and the Rule of Law', in N. O'Sullivan (ed.), *Terrorism, Ideology and Revolution*, Wheatsheaf, Brighton, Sussex, 1986, pp. 205–24.

Wittgenstein, Ludwig, *On Certainty*, trans. by D. Paul and G. E. M Anscombe, and ed. by G. E. M. Anscombe and G. H. Wright, Basil Blackwell, Oxford, 1969.

Woddis, Roger, 'Ethics for Everyman', *The New Oxford Book of Light Verse*, Oxford University Press, Oxford, 1978.

Yeager, Chuck, *Yeager: An Autobiography*, ed. by Leo Janos, Bantam, New York, 1986.

Young, Robert, 'Revolutionary Terrorism, Crime and Morality', *Social Theory and Practice*, vol. 4, 1977, pp. 287–302.

Index